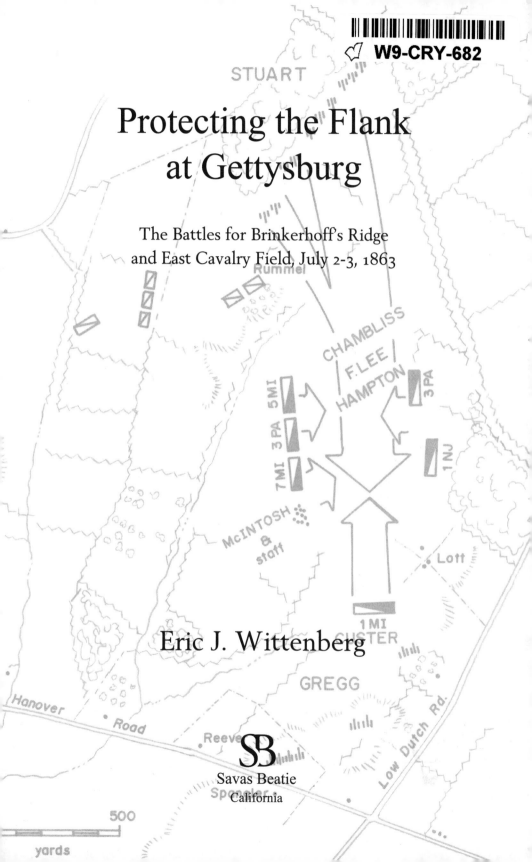

Protecting the Flank at Gettysburg

The Battles for Brinkerhoff's Ridge
and East Cavalry Field, July 2-3, 1863

Eric J. Wittenberg

SB

Savas Beatie
California

Originally published as *Protecting the Flanks: The Battles for Brinkerhoff's Ridge and East Cavalry Field, Battle of Gettysburg, July 2-3, 1863* (Ironclad Publishing, 2002).

Library of Congress Cataloging-in-Publication Data

Wittenberg, Eric J., 1961-
[Protecting the Flank]
Protecting the Flank at Gettysburg : the Battles for Brinkerhoff's Ridge and East Cavalry Field, July 2-3, 1863 / Eric J. Wittenberg. — First Savas Beatie edition, completely revised and expanded.
  pages cm
Original title: Protecting the flank.
Includes bibliographical references and index.
ISBN 978-1-61121-094-1
  1. Gettysburg, Battle of, Gettysburg, Pa., 1863. 2. Pennsylvania—History—Civil War, 1861-1865—Cavalry operations. 3. United States—History—Civil War, 1861-1865—Cavalry operations. I. Title.
E475.53.W76 2013
973.7'349—dc23
2012051775

SB

Published by
Savas Beatie LLC
989 Governor Drive, Suite 102
El Dorado Hills, California 95762

Phone: 916-941-6896
E-mail: sales@savasbeatie.com

Savas Beatie titles are available at special discounts for bulk purchases in the United States by corporations, institutions, and other organizations. For more details, please contact Special Sales, P.O. Box 4527, El Dorado Hills, CA 95762, or you may e-mail us at sales@savasbeatie.com, or visit our website at www. savasbeatie.com for additional information.

Printed in the United States of America

This work is respectfully dedicated to the horse soldiers of the Union and Confederacy, who followed their respective guidons into battle on many a field, and to the memory of those men who gave the last full measure of their devotion to the causes they believed in. It is also dedicated to my parents, Joseph and Leah Wittenberg, who have always encouraged me to study and learn.

Other Books by Eric J. Wittenberg

Gettysburg's Forgotten Cavalry Actions (1998, 2011)

We Have it Damned Hard Out Here: The Civil War Letters of Sgt. Thomas W. Smith, Sixth Pennsylvania Cavalry (1999)

One of Custer's Wolverines: The Civil War Letters of Brevet Brigadier General James H. Kidd, 6th Michigan Cavalry (2000)

Under Custer's Command: The Civil War Journal of James Henry Avery (2000)

At Custer's Side: The Civil War Writings of James Harvey Kidd (2001)

Glory Enough for All: Sheridan's Second Raid and the Battle of Trevilian Station (2001)

With Sheridan in the Final Campaign Against Lee (2002)

Little Phil: A Reassessment of the Civil War Leadership of Gen. Philip H. Sheridan (2002)

The Union Cavalry Comes of Age: Hartwood Church to Brandy Station, 1863 (2003)

The Battle of Monroe's Crossroads and the Civil War's Final Campaign (2006)

Plenty of Blame to Go Around: Jeb Stuart's Controversial Ride to Gettysburg (with J. David Petruzzi, 2006)

Rush's Lancers: The Sixth Pennsylvania Cavalry in the Civil War (2007)

One Continuous Fight: The Retreat from Gettysburg and the Pursuit of Lee's Army of Northern Virginia, July 4-14, 1863 (with J. David Petruzzi and Michael F. Nugent, 2008)

Like a Meteor Blazing Brightly: The Short but Controversial Life of Colonel Ulric Dahlgren (2009)

The Battle of Brandy Station: North America's Largest Cavalry Battle (2010)

The Cavalry Charge
by Francis A. Durivage

With bray of the trumpet
And roll of the drum,
And keen ring of bugle,
The cavalry come.
Sharp clank the steel scabbards,
The bridle-chains ring,
And foam from red nostrils
The wild chargers fling.

Tramp! tramp! o'er the greensward
That quivers below,
Scarce held by the curb-bit
The fierce horses go!
And the grim-visaged colonel,
With ear-rending shout,
Peals forth to the squadrons
The order "Trot out!"

One hand on the sabre,
And one on the rein,
The troopers move forward
In line on the plain.
As rings the word "Gallop!"
The steel scabbards clank,
And each rowel is pressed
To a horse's hot flank:
And swift is their rush
As the wild torrent's flow,
When it pours from the crag
On the valley below.

"Charge!" thunders the leader:
Like shaft from the bow
Each mad horse is hurled
On the wavering foe.

A thousand bright sabres
Are gleaming in air;
A thousand dark horses
Are dashed on the square.

Resistless and reckless
Of aught may betide,
Like demons, not mortals,
The wild troopers ride.
Cut right! and cut left!
For the parry who needs?
The bayonets shiver
Like wind-shattered reeds.
Vain – vain the red volley
That bursts from the square,
The random-shot bullets
Are wasted in air.
Triumphant, remorseless,
Unerring as death,
No sabre that's stainless
Returns to its sheath.

The wounds that are dealt
By that murderous steel
Will never yield case
For the surgeon to heal.
Hurrah! they are broken
Hurrah! boys, they fly
None linger save those
Who but linger to die.

Contents

Contents (continued)

Maps and photos have been placed throughout the text
for the convenience of the reader

Preface to the 2002 Edition

I have devoted much of my adult life to the study of cavalry operations in the Gettysburg campaign. Few aspects of the pivotal campaign of the Civil War have held my attention more raptly, or longer, than have the intricate chess games played by the horse soldiers of the Army of the Potomac and the Army of Northern Virginia. Nowhere is the intricacy of that chess game more obvious than it was on the East Cavalry Field at Gettysburg on July 3, 1863. I hope to tell the stories of the men who fought there, and also to provide a useful driving tour guide of the many important sites associated with this action.

However, in order to understand fully the fighting on East Cavalry Field, the reader must first understand the fighting on nearby Brinkerhoff's Ridge late on the afternoon of July 2. But for the fighting on Brinkerhoff's Ridge, it is quite likely that the battle for the East Cavalry Field would not have taken place. I also tell that story and place the battle for Brinkerhoff's Ridge in its proper context. The ferocious dismounted fighting between the Confederates of Jenkins's Brigade and the men of the 5th Michigan Cavalry has not received proper attention, and I intend to rectify that with this work. The story of the heroic stand and fight by Maj. Noah H. Ferry and his Wolverines against the severe fire laid down by the men of Lt. Col. Vincent A. Witcher's 34th Battalion of Virginia Cavalry has never been adequately told.

Upon completing the narrative, and after taking the driving tour laid out in this book, you, the reader, will have a much better understanding and appreciation of the ordeal of the Union and Confederate horse soldiers on those two hot, dry days at Gettysburg. Wherever possible, I allow the soldiers to tell their own stories. I also provide numerous maps and other illustrations to bring these faceless men to life. Finally, I have also included a number of modern-day views of the relevant sites, both to give the reader an idea of what the area looks like today, but also to provide landmarks for the driving tour.

As with every project of this nature, I owe a deep debt of gratitude to a number of people. Bernadette Adkins inspired me to complete this project. I am also grateful to John C. Heiser for gracing this book with his wonderfully detailed maps. Likewise, I appreciate D. Scott Hartwig's insightful comments on the manuscript. My friend and fellow historian Jeffry D. Wert reviewed the manuscript and provided useful comments, as did Col. Jerry F. Meyers, U.S. Army (retired). Jerry also planted the seed in my mind that Jeb Stuart had other objectives for his foray to the East Cavalry Field, and I am grateful to him for sharing his theory with me. I am grateful to Jerry for sharing his ideas with me, and for allowing me to explore them here.

Edward G. Longacre, the noted cavalry historian, reviewed my work and wrote the Foreword that follows. Sal Prezioso assisted me in laying out the driving tour set forth herein, and Sal kindly allowed me to use his handsome home Red Patch as a working headquarters during my trips to visit the field. J. David Petruzzi, my friend and fellow student of Gettysburg's cavalry actions, reviewed the manuscript and gave me suggestions as to how to improve it. Tonia J. Smith of Pinehurst, North Carolina, shared her insights into the manuscript and gave me the Southern perspective on the fighting on East Cavalry Field.

Prof. Terry L. Jones, of Northeastern Louisiana University, generously provided me with a photograph of Maj. Campbell Brown, and also provided with me an advance copy of the Gettysburg chapter of his book of Brown's writings on the Civil War. Likewise, Ben Ritter of Winchester, Virginia, provided an image of Col. John Q. A. Nadenbousch of the 2nd Virginia Infantry. Randy Hackenberg of the United States Military History Institute also assisted with the selection of illustrations for this project, and I am grateful for Randy's help.

My editor, David Wieck, did a fine job of handling this manuscript and in shepherding it through the labyrinthine process of bringing a book to life.

Likewise, the good folks at Ironclad Publishing did a fine job of making this book what it is. I appreciate their efforts.

Most importantly, and as always, I am most indebted to my wife, best friend, and traveling companion, Susan Skilken Wittenberg. Susan has endless patience with my addiction to the stories of the horse soldiers of the Civil War, and I could not accomplish the things that I do without her unconditional love and unflinching support.

As always, thank you, Susan.

Eric J. Wittenberg
Columbus, Ohio

Preface to the 2013 Edition

It's always fun to revisit an old friend years after a last visit. In this instance, I wrote this book more than a decade ago, and since that time have uncovered new primary source material I did not have for the first edition. In particular, I located the full reports of the regiments of Brig. Gen. George A. Custer's Michigan Cavalry Brigade, and also Custer's own report of the fighting on East Cavalry Field, which does not appear in the *Official Records* of the Civil War. Being able to add this new material—along with other new items of primary source material—means that I am now able to tell this story in a more complete way, and also to address some other new issues that were not covered in the original edition. I have also added another of John Heiser's maps to help interpret the events that took place on East Cavalry Field. When Ted Savas of Savas Beatie offered me the chance to bring out a new expanded and completely revised edition of what has always been one of my favorite works, I jumped at that opportunity. I'm pleased to present this new edition, and hope you enjoy it as much as I enjoyed preparing it.

When I first wrote this book, few people had GPS units in their cars. I certainly didn't. However, since then many cars have them built in, many people have acquired after-market GPS units, and most smart phones now have or offer GPS software. Because the original version of this book pre-dated my ownership of a GPS, I have added GPS coordinates to the driving/walking tour at the back of the book. In addition, the National Park

Service has built and opened a new Visitor's Center (and has torn down the old one), so the directions in the original book are no longer accurate and require revision to reflect these changes. The driving/walking tour addresses the new Visitor's Center, includes GPS coordinates, and also includes new photographs of the contemporary views of Brinkerhoff's Ridge and East Cavalry Field.

In 2005, Tom Carhart published a book called *Lost Triumph: Lee's Real Plan at Gettysburg and Why It Failed.* In that book, Carhart postulates that Jeb Stuart was to coordinate an attack on the Union rear with the Pickett-Pettigrew-Trimble infantry assault on the Army of the Potomac's center on Cemetery Ridge. He claims the four shots fired by Stuart's artillery at the beginning of the fighting on East Cavalry Field were intended to be a signal to Lee that Stuart's troopers were in place and ready to attack. Finally, Carhart gives all the credit for the Union victory on East Cavalry Field to Custer and not Brig. Gen. David M. Gregg, the overall Union commander. Carhart's book is in my opinion controversial, and lacks credible support in the historical evidence. As a result, I decided to address the issue of Stuart's real mission on East Cavalry Field, which readers will find in Appendix C. My hope is that this settles the issue once and for all.

A second controversy is the identity of the Confederate battery that fired those four shots at the beginning of the fighting on East Cavalry Field. This issue is addressed in Appendix D.

Acknowledgments

As always, and with every project of this nature, I have many people to thank for their assistance, and I sincerely hope that nobody will be offended if I inadvertently leave someone off this list. As is often the case, I am grateful to my dear friend and writing partner J. David Petruzzi for his unselfish sharing of good information with me, as he so often does. J.D. also read the draft of this revised edition and gave me valuable feedback.

Gettysburg Licensed Battlefield Guide and part-time East Cavalry Field resident Stan O'Donnell also read the manuscript and acted as a sounding board as I worked out the issue of which Confederate battery fired the first shots on East Cavalry Field.

Robert J. Trout, *the* authority on the Army of Northern Virginia's horse artillery, provided me with useful insight into these gunners and the reasons why Stuart fired multiple artillery shots at the beginning of the fighting on East Cavalry Field. Craig Swain likewise provided me with good food for thought about the same issue.

Researcher and author Bryce A. Suderow, as he so often does, obtained some of the new primary source material that appears in this book for me, and I very much appreciate his help.

I likewise am grateful to Theodore P. Savas and the rest of the crew at Savas Beatie for giving me this opportunity to revise and repackage this book. Savas Beatie always does a great job with its Civil War books, and I am honored to be part of the company's stable of writers.

And finally, I continue to owe the largest debt of gratitude to my much loved but long-suffering wife, Susan Skilken Wittenberg, who not only understands my compulsive need to tell the stories of Civil War cavalrymen, she regularly encourages me to do so. I could not accomplish what I do without her love and support.

Eric J. Wittenberg
Columbus, Ohio

Foreword

Historians agree that the Gettysburg campaign of June 3 through July 14, 1863, witnessed the zenith of cavalry warfare on the North American continent. That campaign featured several notable clashes between the mounted forces of Confederate Major General James Ewell Brown ("Jeb") Stuart and Union Brigadier General (later Major General) Alfred Pleasonton, including Brandy Station (June 9), Aldie (June 17), Middleburg (June 19), Upperville (June 21), Hanover (June 30), and Hunterstown (July 2). In each of these engagements the opposing cavalries fought bravely and well, demonstrated inspired tactics, and suffered heavy casualties, giving the lie to the premise behind a famous early-war jibe, "Whoever saw a dead cavalryman?"

Arguably, the most significant clash during this period occurred on the fields and ridges three and a half miles east of the village of Gettysburg, Pennsylvania, on the sultry afternoon of July 3. That day the opposing horsemen fought with a ferocity and desperation rarely displayed by troops of any army. The fighting made notable the names of such landmarks as Brinkerhoff's Ridge, Cress's Ridge, and the Rummel Farm, while conferring renown on Union commanders including David McMurtrie Gregg and George Armstrong Custer, and giving new prominence to Confederate veterans such as Wade Hampton and Fitzhugh Lee. More than merely a showcase for the talents of those who commanded, the mounted fighting near Gettysburg made lasting contributions to the battle, the campaign, and the history of the American cavalry.

Many books and articles have chronicled the dramatic engagement, but most have given it limited coverage, preferring to view it as a minor facet of a great campaign. The present study is the first to tell the story in the depth and detail it deserves. Both as a history of this once forgotten battle- within-a-battle and as a comprehensive guide to the field on which it was fought, it is a story worth reading and remembering.

Edward G. Longacre
author of *The Cavalry at Gettysburg*

Chapter 1

Prelude to Battle

Brigadier General David M. Gregg watched as the Second Division of the Army of the Potomac's Cavalry Corps rode past. Little escaped his critical eye. His men and horses were exhausted, but duty called. A day earlier, John Buford's cavalry had opened a battle in Pennsylvania. Gregg's men were needed.

Gregg's tired horse soldiers had spent nearly four solid days in the saddle by the morning of July 2, 1863, but they still had not reached Gettysburg, Pennsylvania. They had crossed the Potomac River at Edwards Ferry on June 27 and made their way through Maryland in intense heat, with clouds of dust billowing along their line of march. Worn-out horses dropped from over-exertion, and dismounted cavalrymen, new members of the dreaded "Company Q," trudged along carrying their saddles and bridles in the hope of finding new mounts. Some succeeded, but most plodded along through the suffocating heat and thick dust. Others, whose horses were too worn out to keep up, brought up the rear with the division's mule train.[1]

---

1   William Brooke Rawle, ed., *History of the Third Pennsylvania Cavalry in the American Civil War of 1861-1865* (Philadelphia: Franklin Printing Co., 1905), 266; "We had a tedious march to Gettysburg. I was not in the fight at that place but close by it," wrote a 10th New York Cavalry man. "I should have been but my horse played out so I was dismounted and had to go behind with the mule train." Justus G. Matteson to Mary Hatch, July 10, 1863, included in Ron Matteson, ed., *Civil War Campaigns of the 10th New York Cavalry With One Soldier's Personal Correspondence* (Lulu.com: 2007), 120.

Brig. Gen. David M. Gregg.

Library of Congress

The 30-year-old Gregg was the first cousin of Pennsylvania Governor Andrew G. Curtin and especially determined to defend the soil of his home state. He was a career cavalryman. After graduating from West Point in 1855, Gregg served with the First Dragoons along the southwestern frontier and, with the coming of war, received an appointment as captain in the newly formed 6th U.S. Cavalry. On January 24, 1862, he accepted a commission as colonel of the 8th Pennsylvania Cavalry and received a promotion to brigadier general of volunteers on November 29, 1862.[2]

The Union cavalry commander was "tall and spare, of notable activity, capable of the greatest exertion and exposure; gentle in manner but bold and resolute in action. Firm and just in discipline he was a favorite of the troopers and ever held, for he deserved, their affection and entire confidence." Gregg understood the principles of war and was skilled in their application. Endowed "with a natural genius of high order, he [was] universally hailed as the finest type of cavalry leader. A man of unimpeachable personal character, in private life affable and genial but not demonstrative, he fulfilled with modesty and honor all the duties of the citizen and head of an interesting and devoted family." Modesty prevented Gregg from receiving full credit for his many contributions to the development of the Union cavalry, but the troopers knew him to be "brave, prudent, dashing when occasion required dash, and firm as a rock. He was looked upon both as a regimental commander and afterwards as Major-General, as a man in whose hands any troops were safe."[3] The second and third days of the battle of Gettysburg marked Gregg's most important contribution to the Army of the Potomac.

On July 1 Gregg received orders to leave Col. Pennock Huey's brigade to occupy Westminster, Maryland, "for the purpose of guarding the rear of the army and protecting the trains which were to assemble" there.[4] Gregg left Huey's 1,400 troopers and Lt. William D. Fuller's Battery C, 3rd U.S. Artillery at Westminster and continued toward Gettysburg. His two remaining brigades were further weakened by the detachment of the 1st

---

2 Ezra J. Warner, *Generals in Blue: The Lives of the Union Commanders* (Baton Rouge: Louisiana State University Press, 1964), 187-88.

3 "David McMurtrie Gregg," Circular No. 6, Series of 1917, Military Order of the Loyal Legion of the United States, Commandery of Pennsylvania, May 3, 1917, 2; Samuel P. Bates, *Martial Deeds of Pennsylvania* (Philadelphia: T. H. Davis & Co., 1875), 772.

4 Ibid., 265.

Massachusetts Cavalry and the 1st Pennsylvania Cavalry. The Massachusetts troopers had been shredded at Aldie two weeks earlier on June 17, and were now escorting the Army of the Potomac's Sixth Corps headquarters, while the Pennsylvania horsemen served as the escort for the army's Artillery Reserve.

"The day's march was a terrible one; the heat most intense and unendurable," recalled a Marylander about the division's travails on July 1. "Scores of horses fell by the roadside. Dismounted cavalrymen whose horses had fallen struggled along, carrying saddles and bridles, hoping to buy or capture fresh mounts. Every energy was strained in the one direction where they knew the enemy was to be found." Inexperienced artillerists of the 3rd Pennsylvania Heavy Artillery, who had just been attached to Gregg's command a couple of days earlier, begged to be allowed to rest and find something to eat; their imploring cries were ignored.[5]

Gregg's two remaining brigades reached Hanover, Pennsylvania, near midnight on July 1, where they quickly spotted evidence of a cavalry battle that had raged there the previous day. "The streets were barricaded and dead horses lay about in profusion," reported hospital steward Walter Kempster of the 10th New York. Gregg roused local residents to ascertain the way to Gettysburg and to find out what had happened in the streets of the town the day before. "By this time we had become a sorry-looking body of men," recorded an officer of the 3rd Pennsylvania Cavalry, "having been in the saddle day and night almost continuously for over three weeks, without a change of clothing or an opportunity for a general wash; moreover we were much reduced by short rations and exhaustion, and mounted on horses whose bones were plainly visible to the naked eye."[6]

After a brief rest, Gregg's 2,600 troopers remounted and struck out to the southwest on the Littlestown Road. The horsemen navigated their way through the inky blackness, while many men fell asleep in the saddle. Periodically, a dozing trooper fell to the ground with an undignified crash, halting the column until the rudely awakened man could be coaxed back

5   William Gibson, "Address of Captain William Gibson," included in *Report of the State of Maryland Gettysburg Monument Commission to His Excellency E. E. Jackson, Governor of Maryland, June 17th, 1891* (Baltimore: William K. Boyle & Son, 1891), 103.

6   Henry C. Meyer, *Civil War Experiences Under Bayard, Gregg, Kilpatrick, Custer, Raulston, and Newberry 1862, 1863, 1864* (New York: privately published, 1911), 45; Brooke-Rawle, *History of the Third Pennsylvania*, 295.

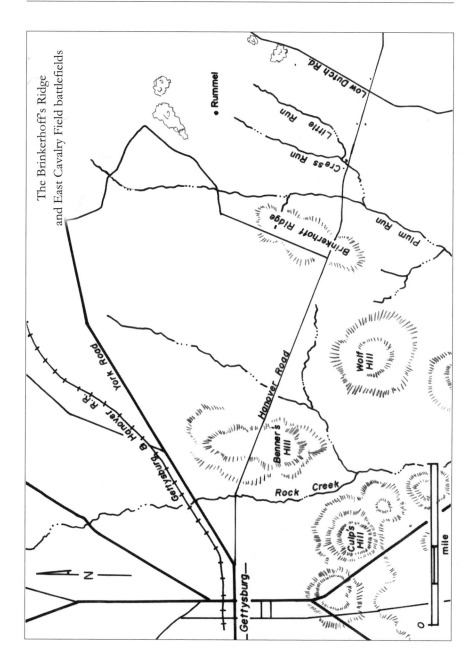

The Brinkerhoff's Ridge and East Cavalry Field battlefields

onto his mount. And so they slowly made their way across the sleeping countryside, the silence broken only by clopping hoof beats. General Gregg and his staff rode ahead, hoping to find headquarters and obtain orders. They arrived at Army of the Potomac's headquarters about noon. After some discussion, Gregg received order to take his division to the far right flank of the army's position.[7]

As the Second Division made its way along the Littlestown Road, a lone rider dashed past the marching column. Dr. Theodore T. Tate, an assistant surgeon with the 3rd Pennsylvania, had lived in Gettysburg before the war broke out, and so he knew the local road network. The doctor found General Gregg and informed him that there was a shorter route available. Within a short time he was leading the men across fields toward McSherrystown. Passing St. Joseph's Academy, Tate turned the column onto the Hanover Road, which ended in Gettysburg ten miles distant. The sound of guns booming to the west spurred the weary horse soldiers on. After nine hard hours in the saddle, the column reached the intersection of the Hanover and Low Dutch roads, an important crossroads about three miles from the town square. It was about noon on July 2.

"Reaching the height, some three miles east of the village, about noon, the Regiment halted and dismounted on the south side of the Hanover Road," reminisced Lt. Noble D. Preston, the 10th New York Cavalry's capable commissary officer. "A rail fence on the opposite side of the road was leveled to give free passage for mounted troops. This had an ominous look and chilled the ardor of some of the men."[8]

One trooper remembered losing his horse on the long hard ride and then catching up with his command about this time. "On the march from Hanover my horse gave out, and I left him with a farmer," explained a sergeant from the 10th New York Cavalry. "When I reached the Regiment it was lying on the left of the Hanover Road, near the cross roads. I obtained permission from Major [Matthew] Avery [commander of the 10th New York] to go to the front, where I hoped to pick up a horse."[9]

"Soon after noon we arrived near the battlefield of Gettysburg, via the Hanover pike," recalled Capt. George Lownsbury of the 10th New York. "We had been sitting on our horses and lying on the ground on the left of the turnpike all afternoon until near sundown." The New Yorkers knew this ground well. The regiment had spent seventy-two days in Gettysburg in

---

7   Meyer, *Civil War Experiences*, 47.

8   Noble D. Preston, *History of the Tenth Regiment of Cavalry New York State Volunteers* (New York: D. Appleton & Co., 1892), 104.

9   Ibid., 111.

1861 training and learning the art of war. They had drilled on the very fields where they now lay sprawled. A few of their comrades rested in nearby Evergreen Cemetery, the first victims of the Civil War to be interred in Gettysburg.[10]

Not long thereafter, Col. J. Irvin Gregg, Brig. Gen. David Gregg's first cousin and commander of the Second Brigade, received orders to ride down the Low Dutch Road to its junction with the Baltimore Pike. Like his younger cousin, 37-year-old Irvin Gregg was a quiet and competent cavalryman. Unlike the general, however, the elder Gregg was not a professional soldier. When war broke out with Mexico in 1846, he enlisted in a Pennsylvania volunteer infantry regiment and quickly became an officer. After honorable service Gregg returned to the iron foundry he owned in Pennsylvania. When the Civil War broke out in 1861, he joined his cousin David in the newly formed 6th U.S. Cavalry with a captain's commission. In November of 1862 he was appointed colonel of the 16th Pennsylvania Cavalry, and served with distinction with that command. In the spring of 1863, he assumed command of a veteran brigade with a well-earned reputation for being "steadfast" and "cool as a clock, looking out from under his broad slouch hat on any phase of battle." The troopers referred to the very tall Irvin Gregg as "Long John."[11]

After the men wheeled onto the Low Dutch Road, the order to proceed was countermanded and Colonel Gregg turned his command around. Infantry of the Army of the Potomac's Fifth Corps blocked the cavalrymen's route, and the horse soldiers were forced to countermarch across farm fields to get back to the intersection of the Hanover and Low Dutch roads. They would not return until nearly three that afternoon. One of Gregg's regiments, the 4th Pennsylvania Cavalry, received orders to cover the army's left flank after the withdrawal of Brig. Gen. John Buford's First Cavalry Division, and did not return until later that evening.[12]

10 For additional information on this interesting episode, see George A. Rummel, III, *72 Days at Gettysburg: Organization of the 10th Regiment, New York Volunteer Cavalry* (Shippensburg, PA: White Mane, 1997).

11 Frederick C. Newhall, *With General Sheridan in Lee's Last Campaign* (Philadelphia: J. B. Lippincott, 1866), 229; Harry W. Pfanz, *Gettysburg: Culp's Hill & Cemetery Hill* (Chapel Hill: University of North Carolina Press, 1993), 161.

12 *The War of the Rebellion: A Compilation of the Official Records of the Union and Confederate Armies*, 128 volumes (Washington, D.C.: United States Government Printing Office, 1889), Series 1, vol. 27, pt. 3, 490 (hereinafter referred to as *OR*. All further

Col. J. Irvin Gregg,
commander, Third Brigade,
Second Cavalry Division.

USAHEC

Another one of Gregg's regiments, the 16th Pennsylvania Cavalry, "marched down to the right of the main line—to occupy a gap and do Sharpshooting-at long range, with our Carbines," wrote a sergeant. "We soon attracted attention, and later an occasional shell fell conspicuously close— but far enough to the rear of us so we suffered no serious harm." By noon, these men were drawing constant enemy fire from several different directions and spent the balance of the afternoon supporting the Federal infantry holding the army's far right flank near Wolf's Hill.

The Pennsylvanians had a clear view of the day's fighting. "The general battle increased in energy—and occasional fierceness," recalled the sergeant, "and by 2 p.m., the cannonading was most terrific and continued til 5 p.m. and was interspersed with musketry—and Charge yells and everything that goes to making up the indescribable battle of the best men on Earth, seemingly in the fight to the finish."[13]

After Gregg's men departed, Col. John Baillie McIntosh set his First Brigade in motion. McIntosh was 34 years old, the son of a Regular Army

---

references are to Series 1, unless otherwise noted). For a detailed discussion of the withdrawal of Buford's division and the detachment of the 4th Pennsylvania Cavalry, see Eric J. Wittenberg, "The Truth About the Withdrawal of Brig. Gen. John Buford's Cavalry, July 2, 1863," *The Gettysburg Magazine* 37 (July 2007): 71-82.

13 James C. Mohr, ed., *The Cormany Diaries: A Northern Family in the Civil War* (Pittsburgh: University of Pittsburgh Press, 1982), 324.

Col. John Baillie McIntosh, commander, First Brigade, Second Cavalry Division.

USAHEC

officer, and known to be "brave to a fault, and kindhearted, yet firm in his bearing when on duty, and a very martinet in discipline." His brother, Rebel Brig. Gen. James M. McIntosh, had been killed in the 1862 Trans- Mississippi battle at Pea Ridge. Although not a West Pointer, McIntosh received a commission as lieutenant in the 2nd U.S. Cavalry in 1861 and compiled a distinguished record of service in the war. He received a brevet to major for his service during the 1862 Peninsula Campaign and was appointed colonel of the 3rd Pennsylvania Cavalry November 1862. With the formation of the Army of the Potomac's Cavalry Corps in the spring of 1863, McIntosh assumed command of Gregg's First Brigade. He was a "born fighter, a strict disciplinarian, a dashing leader, and a polished gentleman," although the men of his brigade did not particularly like him. McIntosh had proved himself a reliable and competent brigade commander.[14]

McIntosh advanced his cavalry brigade a few hundred yards west along the Hanover Road. His command (the 3rd Pennsylvania, 1st New Jersey, and 1st Maryland regiments) advanced to the house of a local farmer named Abraham Little and took up position on the northeastern slope of Cress Ridge along the banks of Little's Run, a small meandering stream that sliced through the nearby fields. The 335 officers and men of Lt. Col. Edward S. Jones's 3rd Pennsylvania held a woodlot on the ridge top above the house.

---

14 Brooke-Rawle, *History of the Third Pennsylvania*, 172; Warner, *Generals in Blue*, 300; Mark M. Boatner, III, *Civil War Dictionary* (New York: David McKay Co., 1959), 534.

They occupied this position until the head of Irvin Gregg's column came up and connected with them. From their position the Pennsylvanians listened to the incessant picket firing of two regiments of Maj. Gen. Henry W. Slocum's Twelfth Corps skirmishing with Rebel infantry holding nearby Brinkerhoff's Ridge about one-quarter mile farther west.

Colonel Patrick R. Guiney commanded the 9th Massachusetts Infantry of the Twelfth Corps. He and his men had been on the skirmish line all morning and early that afternoon. He welcomed the arrival of a large force of cavalry that might relieve him and his command. His relief soon turned to disgust. "I found myself protecting an inactive cavalry force large enough and assuredly brave enough to take care of its own front," wrote a disgusted Guiney in a letter not long after the end of the war. Finally, to Guiney's satisfaction, Colonel Gregg ordered Maj. Matthew H. Avery of the 10th New York Cavalry to send a squadron forward to relieve the exhausted infantrymen and to picket the crest of Brinkerhoff's Ridge. Gregg also instructed Capt. William D. Rank to unlimber his section of two 3-inch ordnance rifles on the Hanover Road at the house of Abraham Reever and to face them toward Brinkerhoff's Ridge. Rank deployed his pieces as companies H and L of the 10th New York Cavalry dismounted and began moving westward along the Hanover Road. "Our regiment were ordered to dismount and go into the woods as carbineers," recalled Kempster.[15]

Captain Rank's battery had been recruited in September 1862. Because of a misunderstanding with the authorities, the men were defrauded out of their bounties and rebelled. Their actions resulted in charges of mutiny and they were sent to Fort Delaware under arrest. The problem was eventually resolved, and the new artillerists were assigned to the defenses of Baltimore. They had only been mounted as horse artillery on May 6, and the action on the Hanover Road was their first combat. One section had remained in Baltimore, meaning that Captain Rank had only one two-gun section of three-inch ordnance rifles with him at Gettysburg.[16]

---

15 Christian G. Samito, ed., *Commanding Boston's Irish Ninth: The Civil War Letters of Colonel Patrick R. Gviney, Ninth Massachusettes Volunteer Infantry* (New York: Fordham University Press, 1998), 201. Rank's other two-gun section (sent to Baltimore for defense) had not yet been returned to him. Preston, *Tenth New York*, 106. Kempster to My Ever Dearest Beloved One, July 10, 1863, Gettysburg National Military Park (GNMP).

16 "Dedication of Monument, Battery H, Third Regiment Pennsylvania Heavy Artillery," *Pennsylvania at Gettysburg*, 2 vols. (Harrisburg, PA: B. Slingerly, 1904), 2:900.

The New Yorkers rode through the John Cress farm. "We met the family vacating the house . . . the women carrying articles of bedding, etc.," wrote Company H's Sgt. Benjamin W. Bonnell. "The man had a bag full of bread, meat, etc., while the children were laden down with hats, bonnets, shawls, boots, shoes, and other wearing apparel. We found some mackerel which they had left in a tub of water at the well. The boys took some of these, but would not take the chickens that were running about. . . . They did not feel like disturbing anything the poor people had left." After their brief sojourn at the Cress home, companies H and L relieved the infantry and "were placed on the right of the Hanover road, on skirmish-line with our left resting on the road, the line extending northerly to a piece of woods."[17]

The other 10 companies of the 10th New York enjoyed a pleasant respite under the shade of some trees. Out of the direct scorching rays of the July sun, they watched what little they could see of the main battle raging a few miles away. Some groomed their tired horses while others permitted the weary animals to graze the rich clover. Others catnapped here and there.

Their pleasant reverie would not last long. The fight for Brinkerhoff's Ridge was about to begin in earnest.

17 Preston, *Tenth New York*, 108.

Chapter 2

The Battle for Brinkerhoff's Ridge

The approach of Brig. Gen. David M. Gregg's Federal cavalry did not go undetected. Confederate infantry pickets spotted the billowing cloud of dust that marked the advance of a large body of cavalry and reported it to Maj. Gen. Edward Johnson, who commanded a division in Lt. Gen. Richard S. Ewell's Second Corps of the Army of Northern Virginia. The arrival of more than 3,000 horsemen posed too great of a threat for Johnson to simply disregard. Johnson had only Brig. Gen. James A. Walker's Stonewall Brigade to oppose the Federal troopers, and the worried division commander was relieved when the approaching enemy stopped to rest at the intersection of the Hanover and Low Dutch roads.

Brigadier General Albert G. Jenkins's Southern cavalry brigade had been operating with Ewell's Second Corps since the Confederates had entered Pennsylvania. These troopers screened Ewell's advance up the Cumberland Valley, and Jenkins's men fought a skirmish on the outskirts of Harrisburg as late as the afternoon of June 30. Jenkins's Virginians were supposed to be screening Ewell's flank on the afternoon of July 2 as well. Jenkins received orders to ride to Johnson's extreme left flank and relieve the infantry brigades of Brig. Gens. William "Extra Billy" Smith and John B. Gordon. However, Jenkins was badly wounded by an artillery shell fragment while standing on Blocher's (Barlow's) Knoll, and Col. Milton J. Ferguson, the second ranking officer in the brigade, assumed command. Ferguson, a battle-scarred 30-year-old lawyer from Wayne County, Virginia (later West

Brig. Gen. Albert Jenkins.
USAHEC

Virginia), commanded the 16th Virginia Cavalry. Ferguson was doing provost duty, herding prisoners of war near General Lee's headquarters on Seminary Ridge when command fell to him. As best as we can tell, the news of Jenkins's wounding never reached him. As a result, his horse soldiers never arrived and never relieved the waiting infantry. This meant that two brigades of veteran infantry and not the horse soldiers that usually performed this critical duty held the flank.[1]

James Walker's legendary Stonewall Brigade, the most famous unit in the Army of Northern Virginia, had only 1,400 men fit for duty at Gettysburg. His men occupied fields to the east of Benner's Hill on the Confederate left flank. Recognizing the threat posed by the Yankee cavalry and without waiting for orders from Johnson, Walker pulled his brigade out of line facing Culp's Hill and turned it about to face in the direction of Hanover. "About 6 p.m.," reported Walker, "our line was advanced in a northerly direction, and took position immediately on the north side of the Hanover Road." His men marched east past the Daniel Lady farm buildings and deployed in the fields of the Henry Brinkerhoff farm, where they could see Gregg's Yankee troopers spread out in a skirmish line in a nearby wheatfield as they slowly advanced toward Brinkerhoff's Ridge. The

---

1   See Paul M. Shevchuk, "The Wounding of Albert Jenkins, July 2, 1863," *Gettysburg: Historical Articles of Lasting Interest*, No. 3 (July 1990), 51-63, and Jack L. Dickinson, *Wayne County, West Virginia in the Civil War* (Huntington, WV: privately published, 2003), 18-20.

A postwar image of Brig. Gen. James A. Walker, commander, Stonewall Brigade.

U.S.AHEC

advance of about fifty of Gregg's dismounted horsemen triggered a response by General Walker.

Walker wrote, "In this position, our left flank being harassed by the enemy's sharpshooters, posted in a wheat-field and wood, I ordered Colonel [John Quincy Adams] Nadenbousch with his regiment (the Second Virginia) to clear the field, and advance into the wood, and ascertain, if possible, what force the enemy had at that point."[2]

John Nadenbousch, wrote one who knew him, "was full of energy and industry and was a prominent citizen long before the war blew its bugle blasts." He "won his way by bravery to the head of the 2nd Virginia Infantry in Stonewall Jackson's brigade." Nadenbousch was "respected as a gallant soldier and officer [and was] intelligent, fearless and persevering" by nature. Nadenbousch, the thirty-nine-year-old former mayor of Martinsburg, West Virginia, marched his 333 officers and men toward the base of the ridge.[3]

Nadenbousch's Virginians were moving off when Maj. Gen. James Ewell Brown (Jeb) Stuart, commander of the Army of Northern Virginia's cavalry, arrived on Brinkerhoff's Ridge. Stuart, whose exhausted men had been riding and fighting for days, rode out to evaluate the situation along Ewell's flank. He passed through Walker's main line of battle and took up a position in advance of the 2nd Virginia's left flank as it moved out.

---

2   *OR* 27, pt. 2, 518.

3   Obituary of John Quincy Adams Nadenbousch, *Martinsburg Independent*, September 17, 1892.

Stuart had a fine view of Gregg's deployments and sat quietly watching until a group of staff officers rode up and joined him. Among them was Maj. Campbell Brown, Ewell's adjutant whose mother had married General Ewell. Brown had been dispatched by the general to find Stuart in order to learn the status of affairs. After Brown found the cavalryman, the two officers sat and watched a squadron of the 10th New York deploy in the wheat fields below.[4]

Nadenbousch quickly realized that the Yankee force facing him was cavalry and not the Twelfth Corps infantry contingent he initially feared. As a result, his butternut infantry grew more daring, harassing the New Yorkers with incessant sniper fire. The Confederates advanced down the hill, pressing Maj. John H. Kemper's squadron of the 10th New York Cavalry. "A larger body of the enemy's troops advancing then drove our boys steadily but slowly out of the woods," recounted a member of the 10th New York.[5]

Irvin Gregg responded by ordering Major Avery to send an additional fifty men to Kemper's aid to "clear the front."[6]

The reinforcements moved out, and the action began to intensify. Captain William E. Miller of Company H of the 3rd Pennsylvania watched the action develop. As the New Yorkers fanned out, he later wrote, "there

Col. John Q. A. Nadenbousch, commander, 2nd Virginia Infantry, Stonewall Brigade.

Ben Ritter

4   Terry L. Jones, ed., *Campbell Brown's Civil War: With Ewell and the Army of Northern Virginia* (Baton Rouge: Louisiana State University Press, 2001), 219.

5   Kempster to My Ever Dearest Beloved One, July 10, 1863, GNMP.

6   Preston, *Tenth New York*, 107.

appeared in the road on the top of Brinkerhoff's Ridge, about three-fourths of a mile distant from the Reever house, a number of mounted men, who seemed to be making observations." Almost certainly the mounted men Miller saw were Stuart and his staff officers.

A moment later, Dr. Theodore Tate, the surgeon of the 3rd Pennsylvania, topped the rise and galloped toward the Union line chased by a party of Confederate horsemen. Tate, born and raised in Gettysburg, was trying to enter the town to visit his wife and children when he found his way blocked by Southern horse soldiers of Jenkins's command, who were out searching for the right flank of the Army of the Potomac. In response, Gregg "ordered [Capt. William D.] Rank to send them a 'feeler,' which he did in the most approved style, the two shells bursting in their midst, and scattering the party like chaff in a windstorm."[7]

Captain Rank was in the process of executing his order to throw a "feeler" at the enemy when "a woman came out of the stone house down in the ravine and began ascending the steep hill toward us; as the gun was discharged and the shell went high over her head, she went over backwards as suddenly as if she had been shot."[8] The old woman picked herself up, continued the account, and went "running across the fields with as much activity as a girl in her teens, without crutch or cane, and shrieking with all her might." The proximity of Rank's well- placed artillery rounds had "temporarily cured her of her infirmities."[9]

Laughing, Rank's gunners maintained a lively and effective fire in support of the dismounted horse soldiers. Their accurate fire caused Nadenbousch's Virginians to fall back behind the protection of the hill immediately. "Such a skedaddle as [the Rebels] made, flying for their lives," observed a New Yorker.[10] These were the first shots fired in combat by

7   William E. Miller to John B. Bachelder, March 29, 1886, included in David L. and Audrey J. Ladd, eds., *The Bachelder Papers*, 3 vols. (Dayton, OH: Morningside, 1994), 2:1,261.

8   D. M. Gilmore, "With General Gregg at Gettysburg," *Glimpses of the Nation's Struggle*, 4th Series, Military Order of the Loyal Legion of the United States, Minnesota Commandery, Read October 3, 1893, 102.

9   Brooke-Rawle, *History of the Third Pennsylvania*, 267.

10   Gibson, "Address of Captain William Gibson," 103-104; Kempster to My Ever Dearest Beloved One, July 10, 1863.

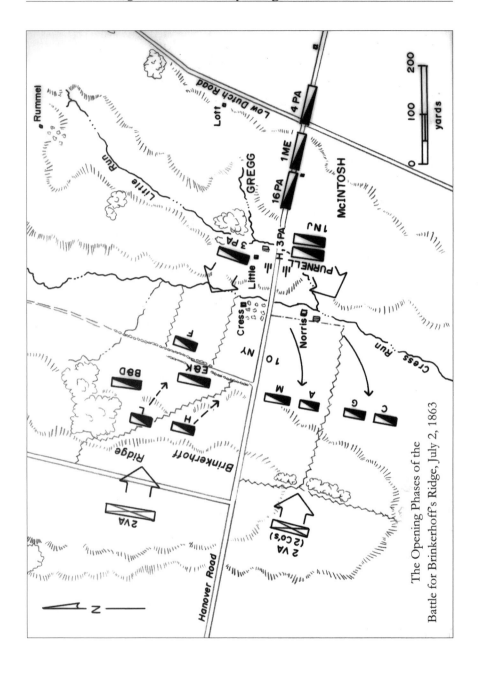

The Opening Phases of the
Battle for Brinkerhoff's Ridge, July 2, 1863

Maj. Campbell Brown, of Lt.
Gen. Richard S. Ewell's staff.

Tennessee State Archives

Rank's gunners. "Here for the first time we heard the roar of our guns with an enemy in front of them," recalled a member of the battery.[11]

Jeb Stuart and Brown, meanwhile, watched Gregg's troop dispositions. Gregg's divisional flag was clearly visible, so they knew they were facing a familiar enemy in the steady Pennsylvanian. Gregg's men fanned out, taking up positions. At first, these dispositions perplexed the onlookers. "Far to our front was a large wood from which at short intervals a squadron or a regiment would debouch, form line or column & cross the plain toward us," recalled Brown. "Stuart, like myself, was quite puzzled for awhile as to their intentions for scarcely any two bodies took the same course. There were three or four detached clumps of wood in the midst of the plain & in these they all disappeared, by different routes. Stuart told me his troops were coming up on our left-rear, but were still some distance, he thought. Presently a squadron moved directly toward us, preceded by two or three scouts. They got so near that we all took to our horses & our vidette got ready to fire & we to run."[12]

It was becoming increasingly clear to Stuart that Gregg's dispositions adequately protected the Union position and supported the forward outposts. Stuart spurred off to find the rest of his command and to reconnoiter the ground along the Confederate far left.

---

11 *Pennsylvania at Gettysburg*, 2:901.

12 Jones, *Campbell Brown's Civil War*, 219.

(Left) Maj. John H. Kemper,
10th New York Cavalry.

(Below) Postwar image of
Capt. Benjamin K. Lownsbury,
10th New York Cavalry.

History of the Tenth Regiment of Cavalry

Nadenbousch sent his skirmishers forward once again. Frustrated by the annoying Yankee fire, he ordered the 2nd Virginia to drive them away. The gray infantry moved out "at a single dash, the men advancing with great spirit."[13] When Major Kemper's small force of New Yorkers saw a line of Rebel infantry forming for an advance, his thin line collapsed. "About 4 p.m. our line was broken by an attack from the rebel infantry, and we fell back across the road to our left," admitted a member of the 10th New York. During this retreat, William Potter of Company H fell wounded. Others, who had taken refuge behind some rocks on the left side of the road, were surrounded and captured. The remaining men of the 10th New

13 Dennis E. Frye, *2nd Virginia Infantry* (Lynchburg, VA: H. E. Howard Co., 1984), 54.

York "fell back a short distance and formed line again on a road running south from the Hanover road."[14]

Seeing Kemper's squadron retreat, Avery sent Capt. Benjamin F. Lownsbury's squadron to their aid. Lownsbury and his men had spent the afternoon basking in the warm sun or sitting mounted to the left of the Hanover Road. Lownsbury was seated near Major Avery cleaning his revolver when a rider arrived with orders from Colonel Gregg, who had grown frustrated by the fact that "my vedettes were considerably annoyed by the enemy's sharpshooters from the hill and woods immediately in my front."[15] Gregg wanted Avery to "send a force to drive back those sharpshooters" on the ridge. Avery turned to Lownsbury and ordered the captain to take his squadron—companies E and K—to reinforce Kemper. Lownsbury immediately dismounted his men, leaving every fourth man to hold the horses, and started forward with twenty-seven troopers. "When we reached the summit of the ridge we came to a rail fence. The sun shone directly into our eyes, rendering it difficult to observe anything going on in front," he recalled, "I ordered the men to lie down for a few moments, until the woods in our front might shade the sun; but just then I noticed some of the mounted men from our regiment going back in the road pretty lively, and concluded they had found something they didn't want."

The renewed attack by the New Yorkers struck within 300 yards of where Brown and Stuart sat watching the unfolding action. "Just when we were

Maj. Matthew Avery,
10th New York Cavalry.
History of the Tenth Regiment of Cavalry

14 Preston, *Tenth New York*, 108.

15 *OR* 27, pt. 1, 977.

expecting a charge," recorded Major Brown, "the squadron turned & moved quickly back, without seeing us at all as far as appeared. Just then a body of Cavalry in the plain, a mile away, moved forward from the shelter of the woods, a piece of horse artillery opened, & a skirmish began, to our great surprise." The two officers watched the action unfold with rapt attention. "The skirmish was a lively one for a time, presently, the Federals returned to the woods," continued Brown, "their gun drew back to a new position & all was quiet. None of our men were yet visible, for in the skirmish, we had only seen the flashes of their guns, not the dismounted men."[16]

Avery fed a third squadron, Companies B and D, into the intensifying fight.[17] This squadron came in on the right of Lownsbury's line, but the companies were small and did not cover much ground. "We were in an open field, and the enemy occupied an old building in our front," recalled a sergeant of Company D. "The only way we could protect ourselves at all was to lie [as] flat on the ground as possible, and every shot from the enemy had the effect of making us flatten ourselves, in imagination, at least, a little more."[18] To make matters worse, the entire 2nd Virginia Infantry was about to descend upon the two small squadrons of dismounted troopers.

Campbell Brown and Jeb Stuart watched the 2nd Virginia sweep forward. Stuart, however, had seen enough. Brigadier General Fitzhugh Lee, Stuart's favorite brigade commander, had sent a courier to the cavalry chieftain reporting that Lee "had got up and was coming down from the heights, a continuation of the same ridge we were on." About 7:00 p.m., Stuart spurred off and made his way northward across a couple of nearby farms, headed toward the York Road. "Gen. Stuart galloped off as soon as the firing began, to rejoin Fitz Lee," recalled Brown, "& I remained fully an hour watching."[19] Stuart went off to ascertain the condition of his command. He had seen something in the lay of the terrain, and he wanted to prepare his weary troopers for action the next day.

As Stuart rode off, the 2nd Virginia Infantrymen pushed forward. With heavy firing ringing around him, Captain Lownsbury realized that his

---

16 Jones, *Campbell Brown's Civil War*, 219-220.

17 Preston, *Tenth New York*, 109.

18 Ibid., 110.

19 Jones, *Campbell Brown's Civil War*, 220.

position could not be held for long. Although he and his men stubbornly resisted the Confederate advance, they were now in serious trouble. His men began falling back, with the Virginians closely following. Corporal Philip Bentzel of Company E was killed when the horse soldiers paused to clear a fence that blocked their route to safety, and Captain Lownsbury received a slight leg wound about the same time. "I was immediately surrounded by a numerous crowd of rebels," recalled the captain, "who escorted me just over the hill to a barn on the right of the Hanover pike, which proved to be General Walker's headquarters."[20]

The Confederates also captured Cpl. Edmund G. Dow of Company K. "As we reached the brow of the hill we encountered a fence, the left of the line striking it first, and we began jumping over," recalled Dow. "As we rose up in clearing the fence we disclosed ourselves to the rebels, who were lying just over the hill, and they opened a rapid fire on us and immediately advanced in greatly superior numbers. As we attempted to fall back we were suddenly surrounded by the rebels and made prisoners." The Virginians marched Dow and Lownsbury directly to General Walker, who interrogated them about the size and strength of their force. Lownsbury declined to answer the general's questions. He recalled that Walker indicated his belief that the Confederates "would win the impending battle, as our troops [Federals] were tired out from forced marches and discouraged by repeated reverses."[21]

Avery now committed Lt. James Matthews and Company F to support Captain Lownsbury's troopers. Matthews and his men reached the top of the ridge and drew heavy fire, the air thick with Confederate bullets. Matthews recognized the position was untenable and "ordered the company to fall back under the brow of the hill," scrambling in search of meager shelter under an increasingly heavy fire.[22]

Frustrated by the lack of progress, Major Avery finally rode out to investigate the noisy engagement in person. When Avery spotted Matthews and his men hunkered down below the crest of the ridge, trying to stay out of the line of fire, the major "came riding up in a rage," recalled Matthews, "and

20 Preston, *Tenth New York*, 109.

21 Ibid., 110.

22 Ibid., 111.

demanded to know who ordered the company back. I told him I did. Just then we received a volley, and the Major commenced to dodge, and he said to me, 'You ought to have done it before.'"[23]

Hospital steward Walter Kempster of the 10th New York had been riding along the Hanover Road at "a lively gait," trying to find a safe haven. The Virginians spotted Kempster, and, as he recalled, "appeared to believe it was important to stop me and it seemed then and now as though every musket in that detachment was fired at me; but riding rapidly down grade the bullets went too high, although many were uncomfortable close." One of Rank's guns belched fire and "in a moment a shrieking shell startled the animal, who jumped to one side and possibly saved me from damage." When Kempster reached safety, one of the artillerists congratulated him on escaping both the enemy muskets and the fire of the Union guns.[24]

The Virginia foot soldiers swept the New Yorkers from north of the Hanover Road. However, Avery's last two squadrons, Companies C, G, A, and M, had assumed positions on the south side of the road. One hundred New Yorkers held a thin line that stretched all the way to nearby Wolf's Hill. These men could hear the sounds of the battle raging north of the road, and they wanted to aid their comrades. Finally, Maj. Alvah D. Waters, commanding the detachment, asked for five volunteers to come with him to "find out whether the enemy were in our front, in force."[25] Sergeant John A. Freer of Company M stepped forward, as did four other hardy souls. The small detail passed through a stand of woods and came to a stout rail fence, beyond which lay an open farm field. The six troopers held their position at the rail fence for about five minute when a line of enemy infantry appeared. "We had just settled down behind the fence when twenty-five or thirty rebs came almost straight for the place we occupied," recalled Freer, "intending to tear down the fence; another party, of about the same number, going toward the cross-fence to our left. The boys were restless and wanted to open

23 Ibid.

24 Walter Kempster, M.D., "The Cavalry at Gettysburg," *War Papers*, vol. 4, Military Order of the Loyal Legion of the United States, Wisconsin Commandery, Read October 1, 1913, 443-444.

25 Preston, *Tenth New York*, 112.

the ball, but I ordered them to hold their fire. When the rebs were within eight or ten rods I gave the order to . . . Give 'em h-l!!"[26]

The little band of New Yorkers rested their carbines on the fence rails and opened fire, their unexpected volley sending the Confederates scurrying to the rear for cover. Freer and his men slammed cartridge after cartridge into their Sharps carbines and maintained a heavy fire until the enemy had pulled back out of sight. The respite, however, was brief. Moments later, "a line of battle was formed, and with their celebrated 'Ki-yi', they charged on us," recounted Freer. "All our carbine ammunition was gone, so I ordered the boys to give them the contents of their revolvers and fall back. When we started it fairly rained lead. I was never in such a shower of bullets before nor since." One of Rank's gunners dropped a well-aimed shell into the midst of the Virginians, giving the New Yorkers a momentary advantage in the run for safety. "The race was kept up until we reached the creek, into which we tumbled, pretty thoroughly exhausted," admitted Freer. "We found our clothes riddled with bullets. One had just grazed the inside of my right leg and lodged in my boot, another struck me on the inside of my left arm, which bled profusely." The sun had nearly dropped behind Brinkerhoff's Ridge, and darkness was but a short time away. Freer had lost track of the rest of the regiment, but he led his little band of men to safety across the farm fields.[27]

Meanwhile, the 10th New York began rallying east of Cress Run. John McIntosh saw that the New Yorkers were in trouble, and he reacted quickly. As Rank's guns belched smoke and flame, the command "To horse!" rang out. The 335 officers and men of the 3rd Pennsylvania Cavalry, advancing at a trot along the Hanover Road, formed a column of squadrons in the orchard behind the Cress house. Two squadrons dismounted and advanced on foot, deploying in a skirmish line along a "strong, well-built stone wall" fronting the eastern slope of Brinkerhoff's Ridge.[28]

McIntosh also deployed the single company of the Purnell Legion (66 officers and men) and two battalions of the 1st New Jersey Cavalry along the stone wall to the south of the Hanover Road. A foot race broke out for possession of the stout stone barrier along the brow of the ridge. The fire of

26 Ibid.

27 Ibid.

28 Gibson, "Address of Captain William Gibson," 104.

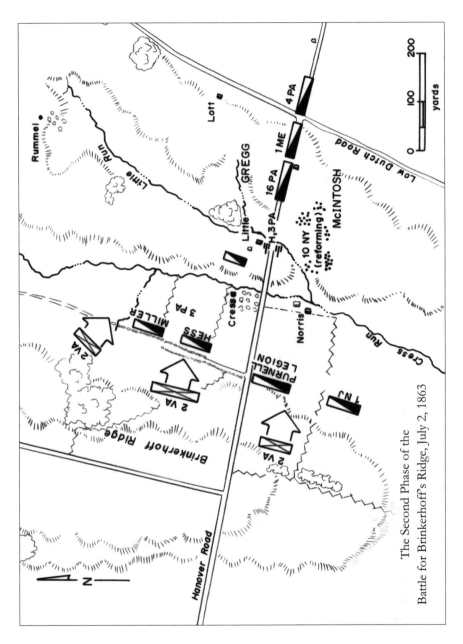

The Second Phase of the
Battle for Brinkerhoff's Ridge, July 2, 1863

Rank's guns had delayed the advance of the Virginians just long enough to give the Pennsylvanians enough of a head start to win the race. Nadenbousch's foot soldiers were a mere twenty paces from the wall when the Pennsylvanians reached the natural breastwork, their carbines belching death at the advancing Southerners. "The wall was the key of the position, as both the enemy and ourselves at once perceived," recalled Lt. William Brooke-Rawle of the 3rd Pennsylvania.[29]

Captain Frank W. Hess's and Capt. William E. Miller's cavalry squadrons deployed at a trot, with Hess's left flank resting on the road and Miller's troopers advancing on Hess's right. On the far side of the road, two battalions of the 1st New Jersey and Capt. Robert E. Duvall's single company of Purnell Legionnaires, with a battalion of Jerseymen held in reserve, formed McIntosh's main line of battle. The soldiers from the Keystone state "punched holes through the wall with their carbines, and behind this formidable breastwork were enabled, though repeatedly charged, to hold their position until daylight disappeared," as Captain Miller later recalled.[30]

Likewise, the 150 men of the 1st New Jersey arrived just before the Virginians, and "the troopers leaped to the ground, and soon, covered by the fences, lay in wait for the advancing enemy. They had not long been in position before a vigorous fire from their skirmishers, a considerable body of the enemy made a resolute advance on them," recalled an officer of the 1st New Jersey. He continued: "From behind the stone walls, taking advantage of every ditch and little inequality in the surface of the ground, the dismounted cavalry poured forth the contents of their carbines.

Maj. Hugh Janeway, commander, 1st New Jersey Cavalry.
LC

29 Brooke-Rawle, *History of the Third Pennsylvania*, 267-268.

30 Miller to Bachelder, March 29, 1886, 2:1,262.

This had the effect of checking the advancing columns and, in fact, of driving back the assailing force."

Major Hugh Janeway, the fearless commander of the Jerseymen, rode from end to end of his line of skirmishers, encouraging the men and directing their fire. "Advancing from point to point, heralding each charge by a cheer which shook the enemy worse than the bullets of their carbines, for more than a hundred yards the First Jersey pushed their little line; and at last, with ammunition exhausted, they still held their ground, facing the rebels with their revolvers."[31] Harassed by the accurate and unanswered fire of Rank's gunners, the Virginians retreated about 200 yards to a sheltered position, where they took cover as darkness fell. Soldiers of both sides maintained a steady fire as best they could.[32]

Colonel Nadenbousch, meanwhile, decided to make one more serious effort to dislodge the stubborn Yankee horse soldiers. He shifted the 2nd Virginia farther left in an effort to outflank Miller's Pennsylvanians. With the Rebel yell piercing the deepening darkness of the summer evening, the Virginians swept forward and crashed into Miller's exposed flank. Miller's end company, holding the far right of the Union line, fell back in confusion, surrendering a portion of the crucial stone wall to the enemy, briefly turning Gregg's right flank. This was the key to the entire position. If the Confederates could hold the stone wall, Gregg's entire position would become untenable. Recognizing the importance of the wall, the men of Company H of the 3rd Pennsylvania mounted a countercharge and regained the position "after considerable trouble," as an officer of the Purnell Legion recalled.[33]

With his gambit having failed and darkness settling over the field, Nadenbousch realized that he had lost the brisk fight for Brinkerhoff's Ridge. Accordingly, about 8:00 p.m., he withdrew his regiment from the ridge and rejoined the rest of Walker's brigade.[34] Nadenbousch left behind two companies, I and K, "to watch the fellows they had just driven off and to

31 Henry R. Pyne, *The History of the First New Jersey Cavalry* (Trenton: J.A. Beecher, 1871), 164.

32 Gibson, "Address of Captain William Gibson," 104.

33 Ibid.; Miller to Bachelder, March 29, 1886, 2:1,262.

34 *OR* 27, pt. 2, 521.

guard the road in the rear of the battle line."[35] His men and officers had conducted themselves well. Nadenbousch later reported that three men fell wounded in the "sharp skirmish with the enemy," but regimental records indicate that at least six men were wounded or captured.[36]

Gregg's Union horse soldiers only held Brinkerhoff's Ridge until about 10:00 p.m. before pulling back to the intersection of the Hanover and Low Dutch roads. From there, they rode on to a position on the Baltimore Pike near White Run Bridge in the rear of Culp's Hill. Wounded men straggled in looking for their regiments.[37] Elements of the 10th New York, which had already had a difficult day, took position on the infantry skirmish lines and spent the night exchanging shots with Confederate infantry.[38] The rest did their best to find something to eat. "That night about 9 o'clock the firing ceased. I obtained a supper of an honest old farmer and remained with our wounded all night on the field," reported hospital steward Kempster.[39]

"Lay on arms to rest-little chance to feed and eat," recalled a weary sergeant of the 16th Pennsylvania Cavalry.[40] The 10th New York, which had borne the brunt of the fighting, left behind two killed, five wounded, and four captured. Rank's rookie gunners performed nobly, saving Tate on the one hand, Freer's men on the other, and assisting greatly in the repulse of the Confederates. "Our action received high praise from the general officers near us; compliments being given to the officers and men without stint," recalled a proud artillerist.[41]

The fighting that afternoon had implications well beyond Brinkerhoff's Ridge. The struggle for the stone wall deprived Richard Ewell of Walker's Stonewall Brigade when Ewell's Second Corps launched its attack against Culp's Hill later that evening. "It was our good fortune to hold them in check

35 Frye, *2nd Virginia*, 54.

36 *OR* 27, pt. 2, 521; John W. Busey and David G. Martin, *Regimental Strengths and Losses at Gettysburg* (Hightstown, NJ: Longstreet House, 1994), 154.

37 Mohr, *The Cormany Diaries*, 324.

38 Noble D. Preston to Col. Hugh Hastings, March 5, 1896, copy in files, Gettysburg National Military Park (GNMP).

39 Kempster to My Ever Dearest Beloved One, July 10, 1863, GNMP.

40 Mohr, *The Cormany Diaries*, 324.

41 *Pennsylvania at Gettysburg*, 2:901.

Maj. Gen. Edward Johnson, commander, Johnson's Division, Second Corps, Army of Northern Virginia.

LC

long enough to prevent them from participating in the assault of Culp's Hill," claimed Captain Miller.[42]

"As our flank and rear would have been entirely uncovered and unprotected in the event of my moving with the rest of the division," wrote General Walker, to whom the need to stay behind had been obvious, "and as our movement must have been made in the full view of the enemy, I deemed it prudent to hold my position until after dark, which I did."[43] As a result, some 1,400 combat-hardened veterans might well have tipped the scale in the desperate struggle for Culp's Hill. "The opposing force was larger and time consumed longer than was anticipated," reported division commander General Johnson, "in consequence of which General Walker did not arrive in time to participate in the assault that night."[44]

The combination of the fighting for Brinkerhoff's Ridge and the failure of Albert Jenkins's cavalry to relieve the infantry brigades of "Extra Billy" Smith and John Gordon deprived General Ewell of 4,100 men, or nearly twenty percent of his corps just as he was preparing for a critical offensive on the evening of July 2. "Could a heavy column of our division have followed this opening and pushed on to the pike, the situation of the enemy would

42 Miller to Bachelder, March 29, 1886, 2:1,262.

43 *OR* 27, pt. 2, 518-519.

44 Ibid., 504.

have been a critical one," correctly observed Maj. Henry Kyd Douglas, of Johnson's staff.[45]

"The threatening position occupied by the cavalrymen and their vigorous fight compelled the Confederate brigade to remain on the ground until too late to participate in the assault [on Culp's Hill], which came so near proving successful, and, which, had it succeeded, would have rendered the heights of Gettysburg untenable," correctly noted an officer of the Purnell Legion.[46] "If Walker's brigade had assisted in the attack upon Culp's Hill, it is more than probable that [Maj. Gen. Edward] Johnson would have gone through [Brig. Gen. George S.] Greene's defenses and forced his way to the rear of Meade's army," hypothesized Kempster years after the war. Of course, such success presupposed that Walker would have been utilized at the right time and place along a very difficult line.[47] For David Gregg, the important thing was that his men had posed such a significant and credible threat that the Confederate army was deprived of one of its finest brigades at a critical moment.

Of equal significance, David Gregg understood the importance of the open, relatively flat plain stretching from Cress Ridge east toward the intersection of the Hanover and Low Dutch roads. So did Jeb Stuart, who, like Gregg, recognized the ground to the east of Cress Ridge as fine terrain for mounted operations. The fighting and keen attention to the lay of the land set the stage for the epic struggle that would come the next day.

45 Henry Kyd Douglas, *I Rode with Stonewall: The War Experiences of the Youngest Member of Jackson's Staff* (Chapel Hill: University of North Carolina Press, 1968), 249.

46 Gibson, "Address of Captain William Gibson," 104.

47 Kempster, "The Cavalry at Gettysburg," 445.

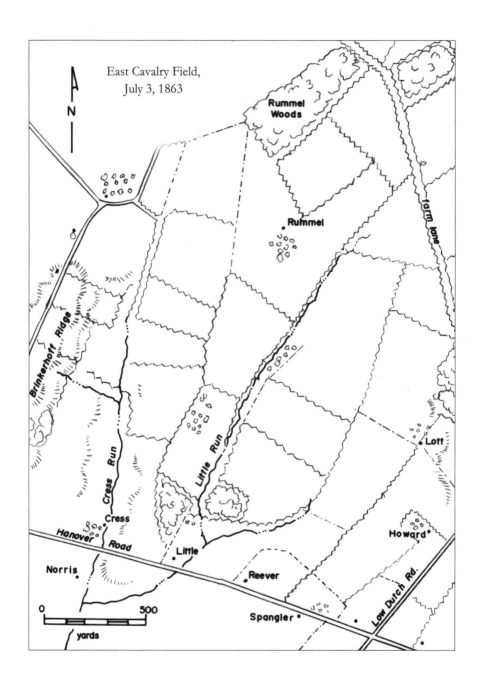

East Cavalry Field,
July 3, 1863

N

Rummel
Woods

farm lane

Rummel

Brinkerhoff Ridge

Lott

Cress Run

Little Run

Cress

Howard

Hanover Road

Little

Norris

Reever

Low Dutch Rd.

0   500

yards

Spangler

Chapter 3

The Fight for the Rummel Farm

Jeb Stuart's Confederate cavalrymen were even more tired than Gregg's Federals. If Gregg's horse soldiers had a difficult march north into Pennsylvania, Stuart's men had it much worse. After a grueling ride through Maryland with 125 captured Yankee wagons in tow, Stuart's men fought a pitched all-day battle with Brig. Gen. Judson Kilpatrick's Third Cavalry Division at Hanover on June 30. That evening, Stuart broke off the engagement and marched farther northeast in search of Ewell's Corps, which he had learned was near Dover (not far from York). Ewell's foot soldiers were already moving on Gettysburg, however, so that information was stale. "Reaching Dover," Stuart reported, "I was unable to find our forces. The most I could learn was that General Early had marched his division in the direction of Shippensburg, which the best information I could get seemed to indicate as the point of concentration of our troops. After as little rest as was compatible with the exhausted condition of the command, we pushed on."[1]

Stuart left Brig. Gen. Wade Hampton's brigade there in charge of the captured wagons before trudging on to Carlisle with his other two brigades. Once there, Brig. Gen. Fitzhugh Lee's troopers burned the Carlisle Barracks. Finally, late into the night of July 1, Stuart learned that the Army of Northern

---

1 *OR* 27, pt. 2, 696.

Virginia had concentrated at Gettysburg and a heavy engagement had been fought that day. Stuart turned south toward Gettysburg. On July 2 at Hunterstown, four miles northeast of Gettysburg, the head of Kilpatrick's column caught up to Hampton's arrival with the wagons and a brief but sharp fight took place that evening until dark. Stuart arrived at Gettysburg in time to witness the opening of the Brinkerhoff's Ridge fight.[2] It was while watching the fighting for possession of Brinkerhoff's Ridge that Stuart noticed the good ground for cavalry operations east of Cress Ridge. "A commanding ridge completely controlled a wide plain of cultivated fields stretching toward Hanover, on the left, and reaching to the base of the mountain spurs, among which the enemy held position," Stuart recounted in his subsequent campaign report.[3]

His men were hungry and worn to the nub. "The regiment has not at any one time taken more than an hour or two to rest, consequently when we arrived at Gettysburg on the night of the 2nd of July," recorded a sergeant of the 2nd Virginia Cavalry, "the men were worn out with hard service and for want of sleep. When the morning of the 3rd of July dawned it found our command in a poor condition to undergo the hardships of a battle with credit either to themselves or their country."[4]

"The utmost verge of endurance by men and horses had been reached, Col. Richard L. T. Beale, commander of the 9th Virginia Cavalry, recalled reporting to Stuart on the night of July 2, "and that whatever the morrow might bring, we feared that neither horses nor men could be used either to march or fight."[5]

Age thirty during the summer of 1863, Maj. Gen. James Ewell Brown Stuart was at the height of his power and fame. After graduating from West Point with the Class of 1854, he chose the cavalry as his branch of service. Stuart fought Indians in the West, including the Cheyenne. He married the

---

2   For a detailed analysis of the trials and tribulations of Stuart's command during its eight-day ride to Gettysburg, as well as of the controversy it generated that still rages today, see Eric J. Wittenberg and J. David Petruzzi, *Plenty of Blame to Go Around: Jeb Stuart's Controversial Ride to Gettysburg* (El Dorado Hills, CA: Savas Beatie, 2006).

3   *OR* 27, pt. 2, 697.

4   C. Chick to Thomas T. Munford, April 13, 1886, *The Bachelder Papers*, 2:1,340.

5   Richard L. T. Beale, *History of the Ninth Virginia Cavalry in the War Between the States* (Richmond: B. H. Johnson Co., 1899), 86.

Maj. Gen. James Ewell Brown Stuart, commander,
Cavalry Division, Army of Northern Virginia.

LC

daughter of Col. Philip St. George Cooke, a ranking officer in the prewar cavalry, cementing his position as an up-and-comer. Stuart also served as Col. Robert E. Lee's aide during the mission to free Harpers Ferry from John Brown's raiders, and in doing so caught the eye of that fine officer. At First Manassas, Stuart made his mark when his 1st Virginia Cavalry charged into Federal infantry on Henry House Hill and helped crumble the Union line. By

Col. John R. Chambliss, Jr.

LC

August 1862, he was in command of all the Army of Northern Virginia's cavalry and had, by the spring of 1863, assumed almost legendary status in both the South and North.

Things began to change that spring, however, and Stuart's vaunted horse soldiers suffered their first defeat in the days just prior to the main early July three-day combat at Gettysburg. Because of his lingering absence from the army Stuart missed the fighting on the first day at Gettysburg and most of the second. He received what some characterized as a humiliating dressing down from General Lee. Like any great competitor, the Southern cavalier looked for an opportunity to redeem himself. That chance arrived on July 3.[6]

Stuart's command on the third day of July consisted of the cavalry brigades of Brig. Gens. Fitzhugh Lee, Wade Hampton, and William H. F. Lee (under Col. John R. Chambliss, Jr.), elements of Brig. Gen. Albert G. Jenkins's brigade (under Lt. Col. Vincent Witcher), and two batteries of horse artillery plus two guns of Capt. Charles A. Green's battery of mounted artillery from Ewell's Second Corps. William H. F. "Rooney" Lee had been badly wounded at Brandy Station on June 9 and captured by a Union cavalry task force at his father-in-law's home in Hanover County, Virginia, north of Richmond. Chambliss, senior colonel of the brigade, assumed command. Thirty-year-old Chambliss was a West Point classmate of Philip H. Sheridan

---

6 Edward G. Longacre, *The Cavalry at Gettysburg: A Tactical Study of Mounted Operations During the Civil War's Pivotal Campaign, 9 June-14 July 1863* (Rutherford, NJ: Fairleigh-Dickinson University Press, 1986), 24-27.

and John Bell Hood and had served in the mounted service during his prewar Regular Army career. He and David Gregg, who already faced each other on several battlefields, had been close friends.[7]

Stuart planned to move east on the York Road to a position where his horsemen could protect Ewell's Second Corps.[8] "The Second Virginia Infantry of Stonewall Brigade held the extreme left," observed Maj. William A. Morgan of the 1st Virginia Cavalry. "The brigades of Jenkins and Chambliss took position to the left and the prolongation of the infantry flank."[9] Two of his batteries, those of Capts. James Breathed and William McGregor were left behind to resupply since they were unable to replenish their ammunition. They were ordered to join the rest of the Southern cavalry as soon as possible.[10]

Some have speculated that Stuart's move toward the Federal right flank was coordinated with the Pickett-Pettigrew-Trimble charge against Cemetery Ridge that afternoon, but neither Stuart's nor Lee's reports support that conclusion. "During this day's operations, I held such a position as not only to render Ewell's left entirely secure, where the firing of my command was mistaken for the enemy, caused some apprehension, but commanded a view of the routes leading to the enemy's rear," reported Stuart. "Had the enemy's main body been dislodged, as was confidently hoped and expected, I was in precisely the right position to discover it and improve the opportunity."[11] The diary of an officer of Jenkins's brigade supports this interpretation: "At 4 o'clock in the morning we mounted horses

---

7 William C. Davis and Julie Hoffman, eds., *The Confederate General*, 6 vols. (New York: The National Historical Society, 1991), 1:172-173. Gregg and Chambliss were destined to fight again. Ironically, when then Brigadier General Chambliss was killed in action in August of 1864, Gregg's troopers inflicted the mortal wound. Gregg returned Chambliss's West Point class ring to his family.

8 Colonel Milton Ferguson, the brigade's senior colonel, was nominally in command of the brigade. However, Ferguson was not with Stuart that day. Along with a contingent of his brigade, Ferguson spent July 3 guarding Federal prisoners of war captured during the first day's fighting at Gettysburg. He would play no role in the fighting on the East Cavalry Field.

9 William A. Morgan, "Desperate Charges: The First Virginia Cavalry at Gettysburg." *Richmond Dispatch*, April 9, 1899.

10 Henry B. McClellan, *The Life and Campaigns of Major-General J.E.B. Stuart* (Boston: Houghton, Mifflin & Co., 1883), 37.

11 *OR* 27, pt. 2, 699.

Lt. Gen. Richard S. Ewell, commander, Second Corps, Army of Northern Virginia.

LC

and, through fields and on byroads advanced to our extreme left, attempting to flank the enemy's army, and to cut off its way of retreat."[12] It is clear from these statements that there was no specific attempt to coordinate Stuart's men and the assault on Cemetery Ridge. Anything Stuart was to do that day was independent of or subsequent to the Pickett-Pettigrew-Trimble assault.

Stuart only intended to cover Ewell's left flank—to prevent Gregg or any other Federal force from dashing around an unguarded flank and into Lee's rear—while also searching for an opportunity to attack the Union rear. In addition, he may have wanted to set an ambush for David Gregg and his Second Division. Stuart could approach from the north, contain Gregg's command with dismounted sharpshooters, and launch a mounted attack from the west to take advantage of the protection of the ridges. He could hide his brigades in the dense woods on Cress Ridge until the last moment.[13] Because Stuart watched Gregg's excellent tactics during the fighting for Brinkerhoff's Ridge, he knew the caliber of the Pennsylvanian's horse soldiers. He had observed the lay of the land and probably believed that, in the course of protecting Ewell's left, he had a prime opportunity to ambush and perhaps cripple Gregg's veteran division. Stuart made his plans and dispositions accordingly.

At six on the morning of July 3, Maj. Gen. Alfred Pleasonton, commander of the Army of the Potomac's Cavalry Corps, instructed Gregg

12 Hermann Schuricht, "Jenkins' Brigade in the Gettysburg Campaign," *Richmond Dispatch*, April 5, 1896.

13 Jerry F. Meyers, "East Cavalry Field at Gettysburg," unpublished manuscript, 3.

Maj. Gen. Alfred Pleasonton,
commander, Cavalry Corps, Army of the Potomac.
LC

Brig. Gen. Judson Kilpatrick, commander, 3rd Cavalry Division, Army of the Potomac. *LC*

to move his division to a position between White Run and Cemetery Hill in the event of a change in the main Union line. If no such change occurred, Gregg was to remain at White Run. "This point is so important that it must be held at all hazards," ordered Pleasonton.[14] However, the astute Gregg recognized that with Buford's division now in Maryland and Kilpatrick's two brigades moving to cover the Union left farther south, his obedience to this order would leave the army's right flank dangerously unguarded. The Low Dutch Road provided a route into the rear of the Army of the Potomac's position, and Gregg knew that leaving the critical road junction unguarded provided a recipe for disaster.

Gregg immediately objected to this order. "I then requested the aide-de-camp to return to General Pleasonton and to state to him that I regarded the situation on the right of our army as exceedingly perilous," he later reported, "that I was familiar with the character of the country east of Brinkerhoff's Ridge, that it was open, and that there were two roads leading toward the Hanover Road to the Baltimore Turnpike; that if these were not covered by a sufficient force of cavalry it would be to invite an attack upon our rear with possibly disastrous results."[15] Gregg returned to his camp to await a response, which was not long in coming. Pleasonton reaffirmed the prior order, but gave Gregg discretion to detach one of Kilpatrick's brigades to the

14 *OR* 27, pt. 3, 502.

15 Ibid.

Hanover Road position—if Gregg was still concerned about covering the army's right flank.

Judson Kilpatrick's two cavalry brigades spent the night of July 2 at Two Taverns. His tired troopers did not establish their bivouac until nearly four in the morning. Major Noah H. Ferry of the 5th Michigan Cavalry turned to his friend and comrade, Maj. Luther S. Trowbridge, and announced, "Come let us lie down and get a little sleep; we shall have plenty to do today." The booms of artillery from the fighting for Culp's Hill soon interrupted their reverie. "That is rather serious music to be lulled to sleep by," joked Major Trowbridge. The two officers curled up under the same blanket and before long fell fast asleep, too exhausted to let the barking artillery keep them awake. About 7:00 a.m., a "sharp but pleasant voice" rang out and woke the sleeping officers. "Come boys turn out, turn out!" called Kilpatrick, "We are all going in today, and we are going to clean 'em out." Kilpatrick turned to Trowbridge: "I couldn't find Custer so thought I'd just turn you out myself." The Wolverines arose, threw down a hasty breakfast, and saddled up. Trowbridge was right: they had a long day ahead of them.[16]

Gregg dispatched one of his staff officers to Two Taverns to locate Kilpatrick. When the aide arrived, he learned that Kilpatrick had moved out at 8:00 a.m., and led one of his two cavalry brigades toward the Union left flank near a rocky wooded prominence called Little Round Top, where the division expected to operate against the Confederate right. Brigadier General Elon J. Farnsworth's brigade had already departed, but the brigade of 23-year-old Brig. Gen. George A. Custer, consisting of the 1st, 5th, 6th, and 7th Michigan Cavalry, along with Lt. Alexander C. M. Pennington's Battery M, 2nd U.S. Artillery, were still there and ready to move. After hearing of Gregg's predicament, Custer started his brigade for the intersection of the Hanover and Low Dutch roads and spurred ahead with the aide.

The Michigan Cavalry Brigade was an interesting command. Two of its regiments, the 1st and 7th Michigan, were trained to fight mounted as "saber" regiments. The 5th and 6th Michigan, however, armed recently with

16 Luther S. Trowbridge to John B. Bachelder, March 5, 1886, *The Bachelder Papers*, 2:1,219.

Brig. Gen. George A. Custer, commander, Michigan Cavalry Brigade.

LC

the new Spencer repeating rifles, fought dismounted like infantry. The "Wolverine Brigade" was a very powerful and effective force.[17]

Custer had only taken command of the brigade a few days before. He graduated at the bottom of his 1861 West Point class, but his remarkable good luck led him into coveted staff positions with generals Philip Kearny and William F. "Baldy" Smith. He was at the Battle of Bull Run in July 1861 and received a choice assignment in May 1862 to the staff of Maj. Gen. George B. McClellan, the first commander of the Army of the Potomac. The brave young officer caught the army commander's eye and McClellan marked him for advancement. After McClellan left the army, Custer joined Pleasonton's staff. His courage leading a pell-mell charge at the Aldie on June 17, 1863, endeared him to the cavalry chief.

On June 28 at Pleasonton's request, Custer (along with two other captains, Elon J. Farnsworth of the 8th Illinois Cavalry and Wesley Merritt of the 2nd U.S. Cavalry) received an unprecedented promotion from brevet captain to brigadier general of volunteers. Custer assumed command of the Michigan Cavalry Brigade on June 30 and made an immediate and lasting impression upon his Wolverines that day in the fighting at Hanover. Captain James H. Kidd of the 6th Michigan documented his first impression of the new brigadier. "Tall, lithe, active, muscular, straight as an Indian and as

---

17 Edward G. Longacre, *Custer and His Wolverines: The Michigan Cavalry Brigade 1861-1865* (Conshohocken, PA: Combined, 1997), 198.

quick in his movements, he had the fair complexion of a school girl," recorded Kidd. "He was clad in a suit of black velvet, elaborately trimmed with gold lace, which ran down the outer seams of his trousers, and almost covered the sleeves of his cavalry jacket. The wide collar of a blue navy shirt was turned down over the collar of his velvet jacket and a necktie of brilliant crimson was tied in a graceful knot at the throat, the long ends falling carelessly in front." Custer wore a soft black hat with a wide brim adorned with a gilt cord and a rosette encircling a silver brigadier general's star. "His golden hair fell in graceful luxuriance nearly or quite to his shoulders, and his upper lip was garnished with a blonde mustache." This exotic get-up made Custer stand out on the field of battle, "the most picturesque figure of the Civil War."[18] He had a logical explanation for his unique appearance. "When I'm in the field," Custer explained, "I want my men to recognize me."[19]

After helping repulse Stuart at Hanover, Custer led a squadron of his Wolverines in a impetuous mounted charge at the battle of Hunterstown on July 2. The "Boy General" had his horse shot out from under him and was nearly captured when the mortally wounded animal fell on top of him, pinning the officer to the ground. Private Norvell F. Churchill of the 1st Michigan Cavalry saved Custer from capture at the last moment. In just three days the new brigadier had earned a reputation for panache and derring-do by leading reckless mounted charges. He would lead many more before the war ended.

Custer deployed his regiments on July 3 in a line covering the intersection of the Hanover and Low Dutch roads and facing northwest toward Cress Ridge— away from the main lines of battle at Gettysburg. The scouts he dispatched to reconnoiter the area reported that all was quiet and there were no enemy troops in the area. The Wolverines sweltered for hours in the heat, which approached 90 degrees that afternoon. By 1:00 p.m., noted one of Custer's officers in his diary, "men and horses are suffering very much for water."[20]

---

18 James H. Kidd, *Personal Recollections of a Cavalryman in Custer's Michigan Brigade* (Ionia, MI: Sentinel Publishing Co., 1908), 129-130.

19 Michael Phipps, *"Come On You Wolverines!": Custer at Gettysburg* (Gettysburg, PA: Farnsworth House Military Impressions, 1995), 16.

20 Jeffry D. Wert, *Gettysburg: Day Three* (New York: Simon & Schuster, 2001), 262.

That morning General David Gregg instructed his cousin Col. John Gregg to move his brigade to the vicinity of General Meade's headquarters on the Taneytown Road. Meade was uncertain of the location of all of Lee's army and wanted cavalry to scout the front.[21] Not long after the troopers moved out, David Gregg caught up to his cousin, informed him the order had been countermanded, and instructed him to return to the position he had held the day before near Brinkerhoff's Ridge. David Gregg was still gravely concerned about the army's vulnerable right flank. John Gregg moved out to obey the order, but soon received another directive to connect his cavalry with the end of the line of the 61st Pennsylvania Infantry of Brig. Gen. Thomas Neill's VI Corps brigade behind Wolf's Hill. "This I did," Gregg wrote, "forming the brigade facing the [Hanover] road, which was about half or three fourths of a mile to the north, and threw forward a line of skirmishers some two or three hundred yards in front, under Captain [Ira] Alexander, of the 16th Pennsylvania Cavalry."[22]

About 1:00 p.m., the cannonade preceding what became known to history as Pickett's Charge erupted over the field. When it ended about an hour later, Colonel Gregg received orders to move most of his command east, mass his brigade, and keep a good look out toward Gettysburg. At all times, his skirmishers remained connected to Neill's skirmishers and kept the Union line intact and unbroken. His men engaged in some heavy skirmishing with Rebel infantry, but they would not be actively involved in the fighting that was to come on the John Rummel farm.[23]

Nevertheless, Colonel Gregg's men did not have an easy assignment. "[W]e were ordered to the Front and Center, but immediately removed to the right of our Center—had some skirmishing," noted a sergeant of the 16th Pennsylvania Cavalry in his diary. "Pretty lively—our squadron almost ran into a Rebel Battery with a Brigade of Cavalry maneuvering in the woods. They didn't want to see us, but moved leftward and we held the woods till

---

21 Col. William E. Doster, commander of the 4th Pennsylvania Cavalry, which had been returned to Gregg on the night of July 2, claimed that his regiment actually rode all the way to Two Taverns—more than 6.5 miles—before receiving orders to turn about and return to the vicinity of the East Cavalry Field battlefield. William E. Doster, *Lincoln and Episodes of the Civil War* (New York: G. P. Putnam's Sons, 1915), 219.

22 J. Irvin Gregg to John B. Bachelder, October 18, 1884, *The Bachelder Papers*, 2:1,074.

23 Preston, *Tenth New York*, 116; Brooke-Rawle, *History of the Third Pennsylvania*, 270.

p.m." While there, Colonel Gregg's horse soldiers even came under fire from Confederate artillery supporting Pickett's Charge. "From 1 1/4 til 4 p.m. there was the heaviest cannonading I ever heard—One constant roar with rising and falling inflections." Things became a bit uncomfortable as the barrage dragged on. "We were picketing in the rear and on the right of it—Many shells came our way—some really quite near—But it was wonderful how few really made our acquaintance," continued the Union sergeant.[24] The importance of the position held by John Gregg's brigade cannot be overstated. "Had General Stuart attempted to pass between our position & Gettysburg, to accomplish his surprise, this 2nd Brigade would have fastened on his flank and held him until joined by the others," observed David Gregg years after the end of the war.[25] John Gregg's horse soldiers held this important position all afternoon, providing insurance to parry any attempted thrust into the Union rear by Stuart's horsemen.

General Gregg, meanwhile, led McIntosh's brigade to the right, toward the low area between Cress Ridge and the Low Dutch Road, and connected with Custer's position at the road intersection. McIntosh halted, dismounted his troopers, and sprawled the men in the fields south of Custer's line along the Hanover Road. McIntosh's troopers rested there until shortly after noon, when General Gregg received a critical message from Pleasonton confirming his worst fear: Maj. Gen. Oliver O. Howard, commander of the Federal XI Corps holding the high ground on Cemetery Hill, reported a large body of Confederate cavalry moving east on the York Road toward the Union right flank. Jeb Stuart was headed their way with more than 4,800 Confederate horse soldiers. Astoundingly, Pleasonton failed to grasp the grave threat posed by the Confederate cavalry and enclosed an order to Gregg to relieve Custer's brigade and send it to rejoin Kilpatrick on the opposite (left) flank.[26]

---

24 Mohr, *The Cormany Diaries*, 325. Colonel Doster of the 4th Pennsylvania Cavalry recalled that "My own regiment is badly shelled, but the enemy is driven in towards the rear." Doster, *Lincoln and Episodes of the Civil War*, 219.

25 David M. Gregg, "The Second Cavalry Division of the Army of the Potomac in the Gettysburg Campaign," unpublished manuscript, David M. Gregg Papers, Manuscripts Division, Library of Congress, Washington, D.C., 14.

26 *OR* 27, pt. 1, 956.

About 1:00 p.m., as the cannonade was opening, McIntosh rode out to consult with Custer at the latter's headquarters south of the Lott house at the northwest corner of the road junction. Custer reported the positions of his pickets and indicated there were Confederates in the woods beyond John Rummel's farm buildings. Armed with this information, McIntosh returned to his brigade to choose its new position while Custer's Wolverines prepared to mount and ride off. McIntosh's troopers moved to the intersection to relieve the Wolverines. His men dismounted while their horses picked at the fields of clover on either side of the road junction.[27] The Michigan men were riding off when the Federals abruptly learned they were not alone. Stuart was riding about two and one-half miles along the York Road, turning south on a crossroad that would lead him directly to the Low Dutch Road. Heavy woods on the Peter Stallsmith farm bordered this road and screened it from sight atop Cress Ridge. Although the heavy woods screened Stuart's advance from probing Union eyes, they also prevented the Confederates from seeing the Federal brigade posted at the intersection of the Hanover and Low Dutch roads.

Stuart held a commanding position atop Cress Ridge. With Jenkins's brigade in the lead and Chambliss's following, Stuart "moved . . . secretly through the woods to a position, and hoped to effect a surprise upon the enemy's rear."[28] Jenkins's and Chambliss's men filtered down the ridge toward John Rummel's farm buildings while Hampton's horsemen followed the farm lane into the thick woods at the northern end of Rummel's 135 acre farm.[29] Fitz Lee's Virginia brigade was the last to arrive on the field. Lee's Virginians took position behind a fence one-half mile from Rummel's large stone and wooden barn.[30] Stuart kept two of his brigades hidden in order to spring a trap on the unsuspecting Federal horse soldiers. He hoped to pin

---

27 William E. Miller to John B. Bachelder, June 8, 1878, *The Bachelder Papers*, 1:652.

28 *OR* 27, pt. 2, 697.

29 Timothy H. Smith, comp., *Farms at Gettysburg: The Fields of Battle* (Gettysburg, PA: Thomas Publications, 2007), 49.

30 Vincent Witcher to Henry B. McClellan, March 16, 1886, *The Bachelder Papers*, 2:1,229; Fitzhugh Lee to Henry B. McClellan, May 7, 1886, ibid., 2:1,376. This stone wall ran along the course of the modern park road cut through East Cavalry Field.

down the enemy with Jenkins's sharpshooters while he shifted Lee's brigade around the Federal flank.[31]

It was about this time that Wade Hampton rode up to Lt. Frank S. Robertson of Stuart's staff in a vain search for the general. Robertson and several other staff officers had also been looking for the Confederate cavalry chieftain. Robertson remembered that Hampton and his aides looked excited. "You must find him [Stuart] and tell him that we have just captured a man belonging to the Sixth Army Corps," Hampton informed Robertson. The prisoner, continued Hampton, "stated that his corps had just arrived and gone into Gettysburg breastworks. It is most important that General Stuart know this." This intelligence also surprised Robertson, who had not realized the Army of the Potomac had received such a substantial reinforcement. Robertson swung into his saddle and rode off to find Stuart. "After about a mile . . . I saw a man on a knoll behind a tree, his back to me, looking intently at something lying beyond," recalled Robertson. "I recognized the General. I went up on the knoll toward him and saw in the plain below what looked like 20,000 cavalry—the whole country was black with them." Stuart listened as his aide relayed Hampton's message and ordered Robertson to ride back as fast as possible with orders for the South Carolinian to keep his cavalry out of sight in the woods and to avoid an engagement. Robertson set his spurs and galloped away, too late to affect what was about to transpire.[32]

Uncertain about what lay in front of him, Stuart ordered Capt. Thomas E. Jackson, commander of the Charlottesville Horse Artillery, to deploy a single gun of his battery and fire shots in the direction of the Hanover Road.[33] Given Stuart's concern about maintaining the secrecy of his position, his reason for firing these shots remain a mystery. For his part, Stuart never explained why he took this action, but Maj. Henry B. McClellan, one of Stuart's staff officers, offered two explanations. His first was to speculate that the discharge of the gun might have been some sort of a prearranged signal between Stuart and Robert E. Lee. This seems highly

31 *OR* 27, pt. 2, 698.

32 Robert J. Trout, ed., *In the Saddle With Stuart: The Story of Frank Smith Robertson of Jeb Stuart's Staff* (Gettysburg, PA: Thomas Publications, 1998), 80-81.

33 McClellan, *The Life and Campaigns of Major-General J.E.B. Stuart*, 338-339. The question of which battery actually fired these shots is an open question, and is the subject of Appendix D to this book.

Maj. Henry B. McClellan,
Jeb Stuart's trusted adjutant and
historian of Stuart's cavalry.

Williams College

unlikely for two reasons. First, Stuart's movement was not coordinated in any way with the Confederate assault on the Union center. Second, the noise of the fighting raging on Culp's Hill (which was between Cress Ridge and General Lee's headquarters on Seminary Ridge six or seven miles distant) would have prevented Lee from hearing isolated cannon shots originating from far in the rear of the Union right flank. After the war, McClellan also told Lt. Alexander C. M. Pennington, who commanded Battery M, 2nd U.S. Artillery attached to Custer's brigade, that Stuart looked in every direction after arriving at Cress Ridge and could not find any sign of the Union troops. It was then, explained McClellan, that Stuart ordered a gun to be fired in different directions in the hope of getting a reply from one of the Union guns, whose smoke he could locate with his field glasses. Jackson's gun fired in one direction, with no response. He then fired in another direction, and finally a third before receiving a reply.[34] Although this seems inconsistent with the objective of maintaining the secrecy of Jenkins's and Chambliss's positions, it is much more logical than the claim that it was a prearranged signal between Stuart and Lee.[35]

Captain James H. Kidd of the 6th Michigan Cavalry, who recorded the history of the Michigan Cavalry Brigade in the years after the war, had a similar opinion about Stuart's purposes in firing the opening gun. "Gregg had been there the day before, and Stuart must at least have suspected, if he

---

34 William B. Styple, ed., *Generals in Bronze: Interviewing the Commanders of the Civil War* (Kearny, NJ: Belle Grove Publishing, 2005), 258-259.

35 McClellan, *The Life and Campaigns of Major-General J.E.B. Stuart*, 338-339.

Capt. James H. Kidd,
commander, Co. I,
6th Michigan Cavalry.

Bentley Historical Library, Univ. of Michigan

did not know, that he would find him there again," observed Kidd. "It is probable that he fired the shots in the hope of drawing out and developing the force that he knew was there, to ascertain how formidable it might be and how great the obstacle in the way of his further progress towards the rear of the union lines."[36] This explanation makes the most sense. And, because it appears clear that Stuart hoped to lay a trap for David Gregg, these cannon shots may have been an invitation for the Pennsylvanian to respond by launching an attack that would fall into Stuart's well-planned ambush.

As we know today, however, Stuart's deployments weren't as secret as he hoped or believed. Major Peter Weber, with a detachment of 50 men of the 6th Michigan Cavalry, was stationed in the woods near the Lott barn. From that point he could look out upon the open country beyond and clearly see Jenkins's and Chambliss's men deploying on the Rummel farm property. Weber promptly withdrew and reported this fact to Custer.[37] In response, Custer ordered Lieutenant Pennington to deploy his guns and open fire. General Gregg rode over to Pennington's guns to find out what was going on, and from that position he could see the whole field in front of him and could direct the battle from there.[38]

36 Kidd, *Personal Recollections*, 143-44.

37 Ibid., 141.

38 Meyer, *Civil War Experiences*, 49.

Lt. Alexander C. M. Pennington,
commander, Battery M,
2nd U.S. Artillery.

LC

Lieutenant Alexander C. M. Pennington was a West Point trained Regular Army artillerist who made his mark on many battlefields of the Civil War. The 25-year-old New Jersey native graduated 18th in the Class of 1860 and was commissioned in the artillery. By the Maryland Campaign in September of 1862 he was in command of Battery M, 2nd U.S. Artillery, which had recently converted to horse artillery (guns that operate with cavalry). His outstanding performance at Brandy Station on June 9, 1863, won him a brevet to captain, and his superb service at Gettysburg was about to earn him another.[39]

Pennington unlimbered four guns between the Hanover Road and the Cornelius Lott farmhouse and two on the south side of the Hanover Road on Custer's order, and opened fire to deadly effect. "The very first shot struck in the Jackson Battery, and they repeated the dose so often that Jackson's Battery was disabled and had to retire and seek shelter," recounted a Virginia

---

39 Francis B. Heitman, *Historical Register and Dictionary of the United States Army, from Its Organization September 29, 1789 to March 2, 1903*, 2 vols. (Washington, D.C.: United States Government Printing Office, 1903), 1:782. Pennington was eventually promoted to captain in the Regular Army in 1864, and was then commissioned colonel of the 3rd New Jersey Cavalry. In the fall of 1864, he assumed command of a brigade of cavalry, and remained in command of that brigade until the end of the war. He received brevets to colonel and brigadier general of volunteers at the end of the Civil War, and remained on active duty in the Regular Army until 1899, when he finally retired with the rank of colonel. He was one of those outstanding professional artillerists who helped the Union win the Civil War.

horse artillerist.[40] Pennington later claimed that his first shot entered the muzzle of one of Jackson's guns, knocked it off its trunions, and broke both wheels.[41] The Union gunners maintained a steady and accurate fire. "For nearly an hour, the air was alive with shells—we lost men and horses, and finally we changed position and dismounted to charge the enemy on foot," recalled an officer of the 14th Virginia Cavalry of Jenkins's Brigade.[42]

As the guns were dueling General Gregg rode up to Custer, who opined that the division commander would soon have quite a fight on his hands. "I think you will find the woods out there full of [Confederates]," Custer suggested.

Gregg, who knew that Custer had been ordered to continue moving to the Federal left flank to join the rest of Kilpatrick's division, offered an out: "Say you never got the message. I need you here."

"I will only be too glad to stay," announced Custer, "if you will give the order." Gregg gave the order, and Custer "was well pleased to remain with his brigade." The two generals fully understood that "the Battle of Gettysburg might be lost right here if Stuart got through to Meade's rear."[43]

To meet the threat posed by the Confederate cavalry's presence, the Wolverines deployed in line of battle facing north this time instead of west. "My line, as it then existed, was shaped like the letter L, the shorter branch formed of the section of Battery [M], Second Artillery, supported by a portion of the Sixth Michigan cavalry on the right, while the Seventh Michigan cavalry, still further to the right and in advance, was held in readiness to repel any attack the enemy might make, coming on the Oxford road," reported Custer. "The Fifth Michigan cavalry was dismounted, and

---

40 Robert J. Trout, ed., *Memoirs of the Stuart Horse Artillery Battalion*, vol. 2: Breathed's and McGregor's Batteries (Knoxville: University of Tennessee Press, 2010), 98.

41 Styple, *Generals in Bronze*, 259. Apparently, Pennington did precisely as he claimed. John Scott of the 5th Virginia Cavalry saw the disabled gun that day: "I saw among other remarkable things a cannon that had been struck in the muzzle by a shell or solid and been 'spread out' in consequence." John Zachary Holladay Scott, "John Zachary Holladay Scott, Confederate Soldier 1861-1865," included in *Confederate Reminiscences and Letters 1861-1865* (Georgia Division United Daughters of the Confederacy, Atlanta, GA, 1998), 7:137.

42 Schuricht, "Jenkins's Brigade in the Gettysburg Campaign."

43 Jay Monaghan, *Custer: The Life of General George Armstrong Custer* (Boston: Little, Brown & Co., 1959), 144.

Col. Russell A. Alger,
commander,
5th Michigan Cavalry.
USAHEC

ordered to take position in front of my centre and left. The First Michigan cavalry was held in column of squadrons to observe the movements of the enemy."[44]

The 5th Michigan, led by Col. Russell Alger, advanced toward the Rummel farm buildings. The Union troopers pushed back Witcher's and Chambliss' skirmishers for nearly half a mile to the edge of the Rummel wood lot on Cress Ridge. The Virginians rallied there and returned fire, in turn driving Alger's men back toward their starting point.[45]

"A battalion of the Sixth Michigan Cavalry, of which mine was the leading squadron, was placed in support and on the left of Pennington's battery," recalled Captain Kidd. "This formed, at first, the short line of the L referred to in Custer's report; but it was subsequently moved farther to the right and faced in the same general direction as the rest of the line, where it remained until the battle ended. Its duty there was to repel any attempt that might be made to capture the battery."[46]

"At Gettysburg, the regiment was ordered to support of the battery," reported Col. George Gray of the 6th Michigan, "four companies being pushed forward in front dismounted" to the west of Little's Run, "four remaining, through a great part of the engagement, mounted and

44 Eric J. Wittenberg, ed., *At Custer's Side: The Civil War Writings of James Harvey Kidd* (Kent, OH: Kent State University Press, 2001), 130.

45 John Robertson, comp., *Michigan in the War* (Lansing: W. S. George & Co., 1882), 578.

46 Kidd, *Personal Recollections*, 144.

Col. George Gray, commander,
6th Michigan Cavalry.

Eric J. Wittenberg

immediately on the left of the battery, exposed to the shot and shell of the enemy's guns. The other companies were engaged as skirmishers to the right and front."[47] Trooper William Baird, a member of the 6th Michigan, remembered, "It was a hot day all around the sun beat down at a fearful rate and the heat of the surroundings was extremely hot. The Heartbeat was hot and strong the blood seemed to boil in every vein. It was the great day of a free nation."[48]

Colonel Gray's Wolverine troopers did not enjoy their role supporting the battery. "On the third day we were engaged part of the time with the enemy's cavalry, and part of the time in supporting some artillery," recalled Lt. Elliott M. Norton of the 6th Michigan. He continued:

> This last is the worst sort of service—to stand still, while every now and then a solid shot will come rolling along like a base-ball, and knock down a 'set of fours' like so many tin soldiers; or a shell may explode just over you, and cut off limbs of trees and drop them on you. This sort of thing tries the nerves of horses and men, you may depend. But there is nothing to do for it but just to close in the gaps made by a horse falling in the ranks, or, wounded, backing frantically clear out of them.

47 E. A. Paul, "Operations of Our Cavalry: The Michigan Cavalry Brigade," *New York Times*, August 6, 1863.

48 William Baird Memoirs, Michigan Historical Collections, Bentley Historical Library, University of Michigan, Ann Arbor.

Despite the difficult circumstances described by Norton, he and the other men of that command stood their ground.[49]

The artillery duel continued as the cavalrymen skirmished, but the accurate fire of the Federal guns soon silenced Jackson's pieces. The Union fire was indeed devastating. According to Lt. Micajah Woods, who commanded a section of Jackson's battery of horse artillery, "The very first shell thrown burst about 40 feet from me, covering me with dirt and a fragment grazed my leg about two inches below my knee, cut my pants and passed on—only bruising the flesh, but scarcely scratching it enough to draw blood." Woods reported that after only ten minutes of suffering at the hands of Pennington's guns, his battalion commander ordered the Southern pieces off the field. "In that time four of the horses at the gun I had taken especial charge had been killed & several had been wounded in my section," he recounted. "Several spokes had been cut by the balls & shells & my carriages were being so injured I could scarcely get them off the field. It is considered very remarkable by all who were near that we did not lose some men when everything else was being struck—only four being wounded."[50]

During those few minutes the Northern gunners killed half of the Southern battery's horses and wounded four men. "The little artillery we used seemed of little service," offered a Virginia officer in what was one of the battle's great understatements, "& I think most of it was soon silenced by the Federals." Lieutenant Woods noted that his battery fired 23 rounds at Pennington's guns, but the Southern cannon could not reach the longer-ranged Federal artillery. "I am confident that had our men remained ten minutes longer all my guns would have been dismounted & many of the men killed."[51]

A two-gun section of the Louisiana Guard Artillery led by Capt. Charles A. Green (normally attached to Ewell's Corps) had been operating with Hampton's brigade since the Hunterstown fight of the previous day. Green's

---

49 Theophilus F. Rodenbough, *The Bravest Five Hundred of '61: Their Noble Deeds Described by Themselves, Together with an Account of Some Gallant Exploits of Our Soldiers in Indian Warfare. How the Medal of Honor was Won* (New York: G. W. Dillingham, 1891), 136.

50 Robert J. Trout, *Galloping Thunder: The Stuart Horse Artillery Battalion* (Mechanicsburg, PA: Stackpole, 2002), 293.

51 Wert, *Gettysburg: Day Three*, 264; Trout, *Galloping Thunder: The Stuart Horse Artillery Battalion*, 293.

Col. Milton J. Ferguson, commander, Jenkins's brigade, Cavalry Division, Army of Northern Virginia.

Terry Lowry

10-pound Parrotts arrived and took position on the spot Jackson's guns had just vacated. Green eventually advanced his pieces to a small ridge near the Rummel barn, but the combination of Pennington's deadly barrage, coupled with the heavy carbine fire of the dismounted Union troopers, drove off the Louisianans.[52]

While Jackson's guns were being driven off the field, McIntosh put the men of the 1st New Jersey into line alongside the Wolverines and took up positions on either side of the Low Dutch Road in the vicinity of the Lott house. The rest of McIntosh's brigade deployed to the north of the Hanover Road. On the other side of the field, Hampton's and Lee's brigades arrived on Cress Ridge. Stuart ordered the troopers to deploy in the fields of the Stallsmith farm north of the intersection and between Cress Ridge and the Low Dutch Road. These two brigades would serve as the anvil against which Witcher and Chambliss would hammer Gregg once Stuart sprung his ambush. Stuart also ordered Witcher to advance and occupy the Rummel farm buildings.

Much of Jenkins's command had been detached to guard prisoners taken on the first two days of the battle. Colonel Milton J. Ferguson commanded the brigade after Jenkins was wounded on July 2, but Ferguson was processing prisoners for the provost marshal and therefore was not present on the field on July 3. Like Jenkins, Ferguson was well respected by the men. "Ferguson was a nobleman of the old school," wrote a soldier of the 16th

---

52 Ibid., 293-294.

Virginia, the regiment led by Ferguson. "He was a soldier, every inch of him, but he had the habit of getting wounded in almost every conflict in which our regiment was concerned."[53] Lieutenant Colonel Vincent Witcher, the commander of the 34th Battalion of Virginia Cavalry, was the brigade's senior officer on the field. Witcher, a 26-year-old lawyer from Wayne County, Virginia, had a "restless disposition as well as a fearless and independent character," and carried the picturesque nickname "Clawhammer" owing to the swallow-tailed coats he favored.[54] Witcher, explained a modern historian, was a tough man from a tough family. "Just prior to the war, his father and other relatives had engaged in a gun and knife fight at a local store over depositions filed in a divorce that they believed sullied the honor of a female extended family member."[55] Witcher "was never so happy as when in the thick of battle as he rode at the head of his battalion in battle charge. . . . He laughed at danger and was always ready to undertake the most hopeless mission. . . . He was brave, hasty, rash and impulsive, his friendship firm and his hatred everlasting."[56]

Witcher had only the 332 men of his own 34th Battalion and eight companies of the 14th and 16th Virginia Cavalry to commit to battle that afternoon, a total of just some 550 troopers to hold a front spanning 300 to 400 yards.[57] Like their leader, the men of the 34th Battalion were a rough lot who served more like mounted infantry than traditional light cavalry. They had not done much regular fighting thus far in the war, and were known as undisciplined ruffians. The other companies drawn from the rest of Jenkins's regiments filed into line of battle alongside Witcher's men. "My company was ordered to the extreme right on the slope of a hill. Our opponents poured a rain of bullets and shells on us but were forced slowly to fall back," recalled

---

53 Nathaniel E. Harris, *Autobiography: The Story of an Old Man's Life with Reminiscences of Seventy-Five Years* (Macon, GA: J. W. Burke Co., 1925), 73.

54 Dickinson, *Wayne County, West Virginia in the Civil War*, 39.

55 Joseph G. Bilby, *A Revolution in Arms: A History of the First Repeating Rifles* (Yardley, PA: Westholme Publishing, 2006), 112-113. His father, Vincent, and Vincent's brother-in-law shot and stabbed the aggrieved husband but were acquitted on grounds of self-defense.

56 Scott C. Cole, *34th (Thirty-Fourth) Battalion Virginia Cavalry* (Lynchburg, VA: H.E. Howard, 1993), 5.

57 Witcher to Bachelder, April 7, 1886, *The Bachelder Papers*, 2:1,293.

Brig. Gen. Fitzhugh Lee, commander, Fitz Lee's Brigade, Cavalry Division, Army of Northern Virginia.

USAHEC

an officer of the 14th Virginia Cavalry. "We lost heavily—Lieutenant Allan, of our regiment was killed at my side."[58] Major Benjamin Eakle, commander of the 14th Virginia, also fell wounded, leaving Capt. Edward E. Bouldin to take command.[59] Stuart also deployed Capt. William M. McGregor's battery along Cress Ridge and the additional guns engaged in counterbattery fire with Pennington's artillerists.[60]

Companies A and D of the 3rd Virginia Cavalry of Fitz Lee's brigade dismounted and fanned out as skirmishers, while most of the rest of Lee's men lounged and watched the action. "During these hours of quietude, I, with a number of comrades was resting under a large cherry tree," recalled Pvt. Richard Ingram of the 3rd Virginia Cavalry, "and had an opportunity rarely afforded a private, of observing the battle which followed." Ingram and his comrades also watched Jenkins's brigade deploy.[61]

The 1st Virginia Cavalry did not get to spend the afternoon resting. Led by Maj. William A. Morgan, who commanded a battalion of the famous regiment, the 130 or so men dismounted to fight and moved forward to attack the advancing Federal troopers with carbines ready. "I ordered an

58 Schuricht, "Jenkins's Brigade in the Gettysburg Campaign."

59 Edward E. Bouldin, "Charlotte Cavalry: A Brief History of the Gallant Command," *Richmond Dispatch*, May 28, 1899.

60 McClellan, *Life and Campaigns: The Life and Campaigns of Major-General J.E.B. Stuart*, 338-339; William M. McGregor to John B. Bachelder, June 9, 1886, *The Bachelder Papers*, 3:1,417.

61 Richard H. Ingram to Henry B. McClellan, April 12, 1886, ibid., 3:1,336.

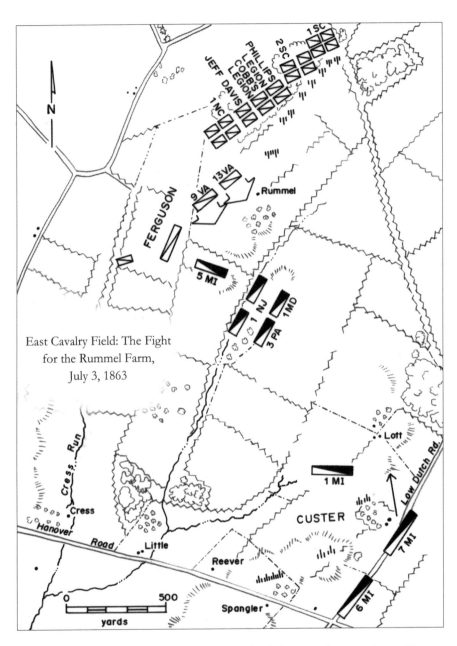

East Cavalry Field: The Fight
for the Rummel Farm,
July 3, 1863

advance on their position at double quick, doing good execution with our
carbines," recalled Morgan. "We continued to advance, skirmishing with
them some three or four hundred yards. On approaching the woods on my
right, I saw a Federal battery wheeling into position. It soon opened us with
grape and canister. I at once ordered the men to charge the guns and shoot the

horses of the limbers." Morgan hoped to disable and capture the guns, but a battle line of dismounted Federals soon appeared on his flank and forced the Virginians to fall back.[62]

Lieutenant John Paul of the 1st Virginia Cavalry and his brother, Peter, were fighting side-by-side on the battle line. To their amazement, the two troopers noticed their younger brother Abe had slid into the line of battle and was fighting between them. Neither trooper was aware their youngest sibling had even joined the army. Peter recognized Abe first and yelled, "What the hell are you doin' here?"

"Nothin'," replied young Abe Paul, "I jes' jined the army."

His first fight proved to be one of the most protracted and bloody cavalry engagements of the entire war.[63]

Witcher led the 332 officers and men of the 34th Battalion forward onto the grounds of the Rummel farm, and many took position in the large wood and stone barn adjacent to the farmhouse. Many knocked out rifle holes in the planking of the barn, which allowed them to fire from complete shelter.

John Rummel was minding his business as the fighting began. "Rummel was in his house and with an army and its horses and cannon invading his yard and garden, was prepared for startling experiences," but what he likely wasn't ready to lose was his personal freedom.[64] The Virginians took him prisoner and held him for the rest of the day. They permitted a panicked Sarah Rummel to leave for the safety of a neighbor's house.[65]

Witcher's dogged little band of Virginians stubbornly held the Rummel farm buildings for most of the afternoon in the face of unrelenting pressure from the Union cavalry. "Repelling assault after assault the Thirty-fourth held its position until our ammunition was exhausted," remembered a proud Witcher.[66] An officer of the 14th Virginia Cavalry recalled that his company connected with the end of Witcher's position near the Rummel farm buildings. "I remember distinctly one of his wounded lying on his face in the

62 Morgan, "Desperate Charges."

63 Robert J. Driver, *1st Virginia Cavalry* (Lynchburg, VA: H. E. Howard Co., 1991), 67.

64 Smith, *Farms at Gettysburg*, 49.

65 Wert, *Gettysburg: Day Three*, 260.

66 Vincent A. Witcher, "Chambersburg Raid: Another Account of that Thrilling Affair," *Richmond Dispatch*, April 30, 1899.

Maj. Myron Beaumont,
1st New Jersey Cavalry.
USAHEC

ploughed ground. When I asked him if I could do anything for him he said, 'Damn you go on into the fight. I will die in a few minutes.' Another with the top of his skull knocked off & I could see his brains. He was sitting up on the branch in our rear. I washed the blood out of his eyes."[67]

McIntosh watched the Confederates advance toward the Rummel barn but could not see Stuart's main line of battle along Cress Ridge. To ascertain the strength of the enemy force facing him, McIntosh dismounted the 1st New Jersey and sent it forward to occupy a fence line along Little's Run. The Jerseymen held their position until they ran out of carbine ammunition and then faced down the Southern horse soldiers with their revolvers. Major Hugh Janeway, who commanded the 1st New Jersey's skirmish line, rode back to find the regimental commander, Maj. Myron Beaumont, to report the plight of Janeway's embattled skirmishers. McIntosh brought up the 3rd Pennsylvania Cavalry to aid Beaumont. The Pennsylvanians deployed behind the main skirmish line of the Jerseymen. When the 1st New Jersey attempted to withdraw, the Confederates advanced on both flanks. McIntosh rode up to Beaumont and said, "Major, where is your regiment?"

"On the skirmish line," responded Beaumont.

McIntosh frowned. "But I ordered them to be relieved."

"The other regiment cannot be got to relieve them," countered Major Beaumont.

"I will see about that," replied McIntosh, "recall your men."

---

67 Account of Lt. Gaines, 14th Virginia Cavalry, copy in files, Gettysburg National Military Park (GNMP).

"I have recalled them, and they won't come," replied the major. Instead of falling back, the Jerseymen borrowed ammunition from the Pennsylvanians and remained on the firing line.[68]

Captain Robert E. Duvall's single company of Marylanders of the Purnell Legion extended McIntosh's skirmish line. The Marylanders took up an L-shaped position, with half of them facing north toward Fitz Lee's and Hampton's men, and the other half facing west toward Witcher's position nested amongst the buildings of the Rummel farm. The valiant Marylanders added their carbines to the storm of lead being laid down by McIntosh's dismounted troopers.[69]

In response, Witcher's men advanced and occupied a parallel rock fence line west of the Rummel barn. "Hat in hand I mounted the stone fence with Captain [Jacob] Baldwin, of Company A, and ordered a charge," recounted Witcher. "The command rushed forward, swept the enemy's line of dismounted men from behind the stone fences in our front, and rushed on to siege the battery." The dismounted horse soldiers traded heavy fire across the open farm fields. Led by the dauntless Witcher, the Virginians headed straight for the Union guns. The appearance of fresh Union horsemen, however, convinced Witcher and his men to retreat to the other side of the fence and the reform in the Rummel farm fields. "Having been 'about faced,' the Thirty-fourth coolly, at the command, 'Take aim,' opened a deadly fire all along the Federal front," continued Witcher. "At the first fire the Federal front went down; at the second and third fires great gaps were made through the whole five ranks. Reaching the fence they had been halted, their front destroyed, and every shot tore through the five squadrons."[70]

When trooper Sam McCargo of Company B of the 14th Virginia was mortally wounded, two others of his regiment tried to carry him to safety. Both men fell wounded almost immediately, prompting company commander Capt. Edwin E. Bouldin to order all who were wounded to remain in place until the firing slackened a bit. When Bouldin's meager supply of ammunition quickly ran out, the captain boldly reported his plight directly to Jeb Stuart, who replied that he had done all he could to obtain

---

68 Pyne, *Ride to Glory*, 132-133.

69 Gibson, "Address of Captain William Gibson," 105.

70 Witcher, "Charlotte Cavalry."

Capt. William W. Rogers (standing, center) commanded a squadron of the 3rd Pennsylvania Cavalry on East Cavalry Field.

John Nesbitt III

additional supplies but that Bouldin's men would have to remain in place under fire without ammunition. The captain was walking back to his company when a spent ball struck him in the stomach. When Stuart saw Bouldin go down, he affirmed that it was of the utmost importance that the 14th Virginia continue to hold that part of his line. Embolden by the general's words, the Virginians hunkered down and held their position in spite of the heavy Federal fire.[71]

Now that the fight had grown into a full-blown battle, McIntosh pushed the rest of his brigade into line, splitting the 3rd Pennsylvania to widen his front against the Confederates. McIntosh sent two dismounted squadrons under Capts. Charles Treichel and William Rogers into line along Little's Run next to the 1st New Jersey. Captains James W. Walsh's and Frank W. Hess's squadrons moved north of the Lott house along the Low Dutch Road. The final squadron under Capt. William E. Miller deployed on the edge of a stand of timber on the Lott farm and extended the line north to the vital crossroads. The 3rd Pennsylvania, therefore, anchored both ends of the 1st New Jersey's line. The single company of the Purnell Legion advanced to Little's Run to the left of Treichel and Rogers.

McIntosh's line now extended from a strip of woods north of the Lott house to a fence near the Rummel springhouse, then toward the Hanover Road, following the meandering route of Little's Run.[72] McIntosh held his remaining regiment, the 1st Maryland Cavalry (a hodgepodge unit of troopers from Maryland, Pennsylvania, and Washington, D.C.), in reserve

71 Edwin E. Bouldin to Benjamin F. Eakle, March 31, 1886, *The Bachelder Papers*, 2:1,271-1,273.

72 Hampton S. Thomas to John B. Bachelder, July 1, 1886, ibid., 3:1,431.

Capt. Alanson M. Randol,
commander, Batteries E and G,
1st U.S. Artillery

LC

behind the Lott house to cover the Union far right flank.[73] "The presence of Colonel McIntosh is everywhere through the brigade to inspire the men," noted a Pennsylvanian.[74]

Because his thin line held such a wide front, McIntosh rode off and reported to General Gregg that he was engaged with a superior force and asked for reinforcements from John Gregg's brigade. General Gregg had held his cousin's brigade in reserve in order to protect the flank, and did not want to pull his other brigade out of line. He refused McIntosh's request and instead directed the guns of 26-year-old Capt. Alanson M. Randol's Battery E, 1st U.S. Artillery, to unlimber along the Hanover Road southwest of the Lott farm buildings near Pennington.[75] Lieutenant James Chester deployed his section of guns on the highest spot in the area. "Our guns being in position

---

73 Daniel Carroll Toomey and Charles Albert Earp, *Marylanders in Blue: The Artillery and the Cavalry* (Baltimore: Toomey Press, 1999), 100.

74 Brooke-Rawle, *Third Pennsylvania Cavalry*, 258.

75 Gregg, "Second Cavalry Division," 15; Brooke-Rawle, *Third Pennsylvania Cavalry*, 274; William E. Miller, "The Cavalry Battle Near Gettysburg," included in Robert U. Johnson and Clarence C. Buel, eds., *Battles and Leaders of the Civil War*, 4 vols. (New York: The Century Co. 1888), 3:402. Like his West Point classmate Pennington, Randol was a career artillerist. He received a brevet to captain for his performance during McClellan's 1862 Peninsula Campaign, and was promoted to captain in the fall of 1862. In December 1864, he was commissioned colonel of the 2nd New York Cavalry, and served in that capacity until the end of the Civil War, earning a brevet to brigadier general of volunteers. He then returned to the artillery, and served honorably in the postwar Regular Army. He died as a major while still on active duty on May 7, 1887. Of particular note, Randol received a brevet to major for his outstanding service at Gettysburg. *Heitman, Historical Register*, 1:815.

we loaded with shrapnel, the first round the shells exploded at the edge of the woods in rear of the line of rebel cavalry that was formed four deep at that part of the field," recalled one of Randol's gunners. "On firing the next round the pieces were set so that the shells exploded in front of the line which resulted in dismounting, killing and wounding several."[76]

Pennington and Randol next directed their gunners to turn their attention to Witcher's men in Rummel's barn, some 2,100 yards away. The severe and effective Federal fire soon made holding the barn untenable.[77] Pennington challenged one of his sergeants, in "forcible language," to dismount one of the enemy guns. "I will try," responded the sergeant as he sighted his piece. When he was satisfied with his aim, he pulled the lanyard and the missile arced across the distance into the muzzle of a Confederate gun, rupturing the barrel. "Well done," said Pennington. "Now try the left gun." The next shot knocked the wheel off the left gun and killed several Southern artillerists.[78]

Lieutenant Frank B. Hamilton, one of Pennington's section commanders, later bragged that he and Lt. Carle Woodruff, another section commander, "did knock to pieces that battery on the slope."[79] Years after the war, Custer stated that, "but for Pennington we would have been licked in that fight, and to . . . Pennington the country owes the fortunate result of the Battle of Gettysburg."[80]

Stuart replied to McIntosh's evolving deployment by sending additional men from Jenkins's and Chambliss's brigades to extend the Confederate line of battle south toward the Hanover Road and outflank the Union position along Little's Run. Custer saw this new threat and sent a portion of the 6th Michigan Cavalry on foot to extend the Union left. When the 1st New Jersey and 3rd Pennsylvania sent back word they were running low on ammunition, Custer also committed the 5th Michigan to the fight. These Wolverines carried the new seven-shot Spencer repeating rifle, which could lay down a

---

76 Daniel Townsend diary, Christopher Densmore collection, Getzville, NY, 46.

77 James Chester to Carle Woodruff, November 27, 1884, *The Bachelder Papers*, 2:1,079; Frank B. Hamilton to Carle Woodruff, December 12, 1884, ibid., 2:1,085.

78 Samuel Harris, *The Michigan Brigade of Cavalry at the Battle of Gettysburg* (Cass City, MI: Co. A, 5th Michigan Cavalry, 1894), 10. This may refer to the gun of Jackson's battery disabled at the beginning of the artillery duel and discussed earlier.

79 Hamilton to Woodruff, *The Bachelder Papers*, 2:1,085.

80 Phipps, *Come On You Wolverines*, 40.

tremendous rate of fire. The 5th Michigan attempted to advance north from the Hanover Road behind the left of the Federal line. Colonel Russell A. Alger, the 5th Michigan's commander, intended to relieve the two regiments of McIntosh's brigade, but they never got the chance.[81] "Dismount to fight," cried Alger as his Wolverines moved to the attack. "Now, men, be steady—be men!" The order echoed among the men of the regiment, who quickly formed into line of battle. "Major Ferry, take charge of the right," bellowed Alger, "Major Trowbridge, take the left! Forward!"[82]

Major Noah H. Ferry, the third son of Rev. William M. and Amanda W. Ferry, was born on Michigan's Mackinaw Island on April 30, 1831. When he was three, his parents moved to Grand Haven, where Noah attended a school run by his aunt. He graduated from Bell's Commercial College in Chicago, "where his clear intellect brought him into honorable notice, and he was chosen to take charge of one of the departments of the college. At his graduation, he took the highest honors of the institution." Ferry married and went into business with his brother Thomas. Together, they laid out the village of Ferryville along the White River. He "spent the remainder of his business life, maturing those qualities of intellect and heart, and that uprightness and business integrity, which made him a universal favorite with those who made his acquaintance." His biographer concluded: "Self-reliant, manly, and generous, kind, sympathizing, wholly above a mean thing, he unconsciously won an almost unlimited control over those around him and in his employ. They trusted his clear-headed judgment implicitly."[83]

Ferry was appointed captain of Company F, 5th Michigan Cavalry on August 14, 1862, and was promoted to major a few months later. Few were surprised by the young man's rapid advance. Ferry's men trusted him implicitly. Within only a few months, "he was an officer better loved than any other. The men had a great deal of confidence in him. We always felt, if he took us into a tight place, he could get us out again. He knew just when and where to take us." That November, the major penned a prophetic letter: "If by the accident of war I should find my end upon the field—for I will not

---

81 Kidd, *Personal Recollections*, 145.

82 John A. Bigelow, "Draw Saber, Charge!," *The National Tribune*, May 27, 1886.

83 Rev. David M. Cooper, *Obituary Discourse on Occasion of the Death of Noah Henry Ferry, Major of the Fifth Michigan Cavalry, Killed at Gettysburg, July 3, 1863* (New York: John F. Trow, 1863), 44.

Maj. Noah H. Ferry,
5th Michigan Cavalry, was killed in
the fight for the Rummel farm.

LC

think it may be in the hospital—
you will have the comfort of
knowing that I have, by dying in
such a cause, not lived in vain,
and that no impure motive had a
voice in bringing me here; nor is
there in my history anything of
which my friends need feel
ashamed."[84]

As the men prepared to go
into the fight, Ferry strode along
his line calmly. He was happy
and cheerful, and encouraged his fellow Wolverines. "Now, boys, if any of
you are unwilling to go forward, you may stay here," he told them. The
Michiganders cheered their gallant major and advanced dismounted through
the thick wheat, "he all the while cheering, encouraging us on; and with our
battery in rear to overshell us, we pressed forward upon the enemy, forcing
back their sharpshooters and battery."[85]

Some of Chambliss's men noticed that the fire of the 1st New Jersey and
the 3rd Pennsylvania had slackened, and that these Northern troopers were
trying to withdraw from the firing line. Chambliss and his men recognized
the opportunity and a portion of Chambliss's brigade attacked the Federal
line. "Now for them before they can reload!" cried the Confederate
officers.[86] Chambliss's Virginians and North Carolinians quickly pinned
down the 1st New Jersey and the 3rd Pennsylvania, which could not
withdraw, and forced the Northerners to turn about and return fire. That

---

84 Ibid., 21, 24.

85 Ibid., 20.

86 Harris, *The Michigan Brigade of Cavalry*, 10.

slowed the Confederate attack, but it did not stop it.[87] Captain William E. Miller's squadron of the 3rd Pennsylvania to the north of the Lott farm buildings deployed his men as skirmishers, "expecting to move to the extreme right of the 1st New Jersey, but before I had time to station my men I was obliged to open fire," wrote Miller. "For a few moments things became so lively that I commenced to wish for more fellows."[88]

Fortunately for the Union, the 5th Michigan arrived in time to meet the attack, and the combined force repulsed Chambliss's attack. The contest was hand-to-hand for a moment. Then, "Alger's men, with their [seven]-shotted carbines, forced their adversaries slowly but surely back, the gray line fighting well, and superior in numbers, but unable to withstand the storm of bullets," recalled Kidd of the 6th Michigan. The Confederates "made a final stand behind the strong line of fences in front of Rummel's and a few hundred yards out from the foot of the slope whereon Stuart's reserves were posted."[89] Although the Wolverines had checked Witcher's men, Jeb Stuart observed "the 34th had made the worst massacre of Alger's command and had piled more dead and wounded men and horses on as little space as he had ever seen on any field."[90]

Stuart's original strategy had not planned for such a protracted and violent dismounted fight. He had hoped to send a mounted column around the Federal flank, but the withdrawal of Witcher's men had forced Stuart to change his plan. "Notwithstanding the favorable results obtained, I would have preferred a different method of attack, as already indicated," Stuart admitted in his report of the battle, "but I soon saw that the entanglement by the force of circumstances narrated was unavoidable, and determined to make the best fight possible."[91]

All the while, the grand cannonade preceding the Pickett-Pettigrew-Trimble assault raged on the main field well to the west. "It has been a ceaseless thunder rivaled by Malvern Hill only in the horrors attending it,"

87 Miller, "The Cavalry Battle Near Gettysburg," 3:403.

88 Brooke-Rawle, *Third Pennsylvania Cavalry*, 306.

89 Kidd, *Personal Recollections*, 146.

90 Cole, *34th Battalion*, 52.

91 *OR* 27, pt. 2, 698.

observed an officer of the 3rd Pennsylvania.[92] Although they had their own fight to contend with, the volume and fury of the barrage took away the breath of the horse soldiers of both sides. "About 1 o'clock there was such a crash of artillery as was never heard before on the Continent," recalled Maj. Luther S. Trowbridge of the 5th Michigan, "Oh it was terrific."[93] "The earth was being shaken almost from center to circumference by the many guns that were being fired on the heights of Gettysburg," recalled a sergeant of the 1st Virginia Cavalry.[94]

Custer commanded Alger to hold his position at all hazards, and the future governor of Michigan complied. "Colonel Alger, commanding the Fifth, assisted by Majors Trowbridge and [Noah] Ferry, of the same regiment, made such admirable disposition of their men behind fences and other defenses, as enabled them to successfully repel the repeated advances of a greatly superior force," observed Custer.[95]

The men of the 5th Michigan deployed in a heavy line of battle and advanced to a fence that ran along the edge of a wheat field in front of a stand of woods. Witcher's men poured volleys into the Wolverines as they advanced, but the heavy fire of their Spencers dislodged and drove the Southerners back. "Our regiment did noble executions," recorded Sgt. Edwin B. Bigelow in his diary that night.[96] "I can assure you the bullets flew thick as hail around us," recounted Major Trowbridge. "I had some narrow escapes—one bullet grazed my pants at my thigh another struck an officer just in front of me—Another struck a rail just before my body while another whizzed close by my head. It was so close that I dropped to the ground instantly and involuntarily and I have no doubt that the man who fired at me thought he had killed me."[97]

---

92 Brooke-Rawle, *Third Pennsylvania Cavalry*, 258.

93 Letter of Luther S. Trowbridge, date unknown, copy in files, Gettysburg National Military Park, Gettysburg, PA (GNMP).

94 B. J. Haden, *Reminiscences of J.E.B. Stuart's Cavalry* (Charlottesville, VA: Progress Publishing Co., n.d.), 24-25.

95 Wittenberg, *At Custer's Side*, 131.

96 Frank L. Klement, ed., "Edwin B. Bigelow: A Michigan Sergeant in the Civil War," *Michigan History*, 38 (Sept. 1954), 221.

97 Trowbridge letter, GNMP.

Low on ammunition, Colonel Witcher spurred his mount to find a fresh supply for his embattled Virginians. After a "fearful ride with death all around me, front and rear, and bullets as numerous in the air as hailstones in a storm," Witcher returned with fresh ammunition for Jenkins's brigade, and ordered the 34th Battalion to retake the position they had abandoned earlier. "With a wild yell the whole line dashed forward, retook the fence and swept the Federal dismounted men back," claimed Witcher. "Seeing the whole line of dismounted men give way, I moved forward with a view of taking a battery in our front and right," Witcher prepared to attack the Federal guns.[98]

It was getting late in the afternoon when the Confederates began to flank the 5th Michigan. (According to Alger, his men held their position until nearly 4:00 p.m.) The Wolverines had to rally on their held horses as the Southern horsemen pursued close behind.[99] "We fell back, not as good line as we would have done later on," recalled Major Trowbridge, "but deliberately and without disorder or confusion." As the 5th Michigan withdrew, an officer approached Trowbridge, "and thinking we were giving ground immediately made a great fuss." Trowbridge reassured him that the Wolverines were falling back only because they were low on ammunition, and not because they lacked the will to stand and fight. This satisfied the officer, who went on to make a rather odd request: He wanted the Michigan men to stop in their tracks and give a rousing cheer before falling back to their horses. Trowbridge rather liked the idea, "and at the word of command the men faced about marched back several rods and gave three ringing cheers."[100]

Major Ferry walked his lines and cheered on his men. A soldier who had been shot down near Ferry cried out, "Major, I feel faint; I am going to die." Ferry looked down at the man and said, "Oh, I guess not; you are all right—only wounded in your arm." The major picked up the man's Spencer rifle, fired a few shots, then turned to his men and yelled, "Rally, boys! Rally for the fence!" Just then, a Confederate ball crashed into Ferry's skull,

---

98 Vincent A. Witcher to John B. Bachelder, March 19, 1886, *The Bachelder Papers*, 2:1,237-1,238.

99 Russell A. Alger to William Brooke-Rawle, November 10, 1864, Russell A. Alger Papers, Bentley Historical Library, University of Michigan, Ann Arbor; Account of Luther S. Trowbridge, *The Bachelder Papers*, 1:128.

100 Luther S. Trowbridge to Russell A. Alger, February 19, 1886, ibid., 2:1,207.

A fanciful woodcut of the death of Maj. Noah H. Ferry, 5th Michigan Cavalry. *Jim McLean*

killing him instantly. He died within 30 yards of Witcher's line. "Our best major was killed on the third," lamented one trooper of the 5th Michigan.[101] "It was no chance shot that took his life, but the well-directed aim of one our common enemies. He died as a soldier should die, doing his whole duty fearlessly," acknowledged Lt. Col. Alleyne C. Litchfield in a letter to Ferry's father.[102]

The troopers in Ferry's demoralized battalion fell back when their ammunition was exhausted. The lamented major's body, however, had to be left on the battlefield. That night, Confederates "pillaged everything they wanted and could find from our dead. They stripped the Major's body of everything but his coat; and cut from this all the buttons and shoulder straps." The next morning following the battle, a detachment of 25 men of the 5th Michigan recovered Ferry's body and buried it in a shallow grave beneath a tree near Custer's headquarters. A few days later, Ferry's father recovered the body and took it home to Michigan for a funeral and a proper burial.[103]

"His death cast a deep gloom upon the entire Brigade," declared Colonel Alger. "He was a gallant soldier, an exemplary man, and his loss was a great blow." In another letter, Alger admitted, "I cannot supply his place." He continued: "every moment brings a sad gloom over all our hearts for the noble Ferry." "We are told that he did not flinch but sacrificed his life in leading his charge," responded Sen. Thomas Ferry, the major's influential brother, to a letter of condolence from an officer of the 5th Michigan Cavalry, "This is our consolation, tho 'twas but what we expected of him. We knew of his bravery and about all of the purity of his devotion to country."[104]

Ferry and his troopers had made quite a stand. At a range of just 30 yards, they managed to fend off Witcher's withering frontal fire and

101 Victor E. Comte to Dear Elise, July 7, 1863, Victor E. Comte letters, Bentley Historical Library, University of Michigan, Ann Arbor.

102 Cooper, *Obituary Discourse*, 23.

103 Ibid., 20-21.

104 Russell A. Alger to the Adjutant General of the Army of the Potomac, July 1, 1863, RG 94, War Records Office, Union Battle Reports, Vol. 27, The National Archives, Washington, D.C.; Robertson, *Michigan in the War*, 585; Thomas W. Ferry to Ebenezer Gould, August 3, 1863, copy in files, Gettysburg National Military Park, Gettysburg, PA (GNMP).

Chambliss's heavy flanking fire, and inflict heavy casualties on Witcher's Confederates. Ferry's valor in leading his men impressed all who witnessed it. Vincent Witcher, for one, never forgot his courage and cool demeanor during this stand, and the sight of Ferry's death at the hands of one of his Virginians lingered with him for the rest of his life. The regiment's steadfastness, in fact, prompted Alger to declare, "the 5th has won an enviable reputation."[105]

James H. Avery, a commissary sergeant with the 5th Michigan, lingered a moment on the line as the rest of the horsemen of his regiment turned back. His decision nearly cost him his life. "As I was walking along on a rising piece of ground, I turned to follow the company, and just as I turned, a ball passed my head. I turned in time to see the smoke of a gun, and a man standing in a field of oats. I raised my gun as if to shoot down a squirrel, and down went Mr. Reb," recalled Avery. "I saw no more of him, so I joined the company."[106]

The 5th Michigan's Lt. Col. Ebenezer Gould ordered Lt. Samuel Harris to assist with the movement of the horses of the dismounted elements of Alger's regiment. Harris rode his mount over to Pennington's pieces, where the battery command asked Harris to remain with him and his gunners to support the embattled battery. Harris reported Pennington's request back to Gould and returned to the battery, where he found Pennington sitting mounted a few feet behind his pieces. Pennington commented that he was glad Harris had come back, since things were growing rather warm along the firing lines.

The young lieutenant had an outstanding view of the fighting by his regiment as he sat on his mount beside Pennington. "Our boys held their fire until the rebs got within less than twenty rods, then they opened on them. After the first volley, the rebel officers called out, 'Now for them before they can reload!' But our boys did not have to stop to reload their Spencers, but gave them a second, third, and a fourth volley," recalled Harris long after the war in his history of the Michigan Brigade. "Many a reb fell, either dead or wounded; the rest were unable to stand the rain of lead and the most of them

105 Witcher to Bachelder, March 19, 1886, *The Bachelder Papers*, 2:1,238; Robertson, *Michigan in the War*, 585.

106 Karla Jean Husby and Eric J. Wittenberg, *Under Custer's Command: The Civil War Journal of James Henry Avery* (Washington, D.C.: Brassey's, 2000), 35.

got back faster than they came. Our boys called out to those nearest to come in or we will shoot; about one hundred did come in." The lieutenant soon rode off toward the rear of the Union line in search of additional ammunition.[107]

Alger recognized the threat to his new position. He sent his bugler, John A. Bigelow, in search of Custer to report that a mounted Confederate regiment could charge around the flank of the 5th Michigan with good prospects for success. Bigelow found Custer and made his report, which set the stage for the drama that followed.[108]

As the fighting around the Rummel farm buildings raged on, Maj. Peter Weber's outpost of the 6th Michigan Cavalry was driven in. Weber's two companies joined the four companies already stationed on the left of Pennington's battery. The major had only received his promotion a few days earlier, and assumed command of the battalion on order of Col. George Gray, the regimental commander. When Weber took his place in front of the leading squadron, he announced to the troopers, "I have seen thousands of rebels over yonder," pointing to the front. "The country over there is full of them."[109]

The Confederates, meanwhile, were pulling back because Randol's and Pennington's gunners rained shells upon John Chambliss's troopers. Witcher's horsemen had exhausted their meager supply of ammunition, which forced the Confederates to abandon the fence line in the Rummel fields and withdraw all the way back to the woods along Cress Ridge. The Federals immediately advanced on their heels and cleared the Rummel farm buildings of remaining enemy soldiers. The Confederates holding Cress Ridge were now exposed to the possibility of being captured. If the Federals could advance in force, they might be able to split Stuart's line of battle in two.

A fitful lull blanketed the smoky battlefield. During the brief respite, the opposing sides worked to consolidate their lines. Officers rode about, examining the field to glean an advantage. Everyone awaited the next move

---

107 Harris, *The Michigan Brigade of Cavalry*, 9-10.

108 Bigelow, "Draw Saber, Charge!"

109 Harris, *The Michigan Brigade of Cavalry*, 9-10.

in what was rapidly becoming an increasingly intricate chess game being played out on the farm fields along Cress Ridge.[110]

110 Ibid., McClellan, *Life and Campaigns The Life and Campaigns of Major-General J.E.B. Stuart*, 337.

Chapter 4

The Battle for East Cavalry Field

Jeb Stuart still wanted to spring his ambush on the Yankees. He hoped to drive the Northerners against the anvil of Witcher's and Chambliss's dismounted men near the Rummel farm with a mounted charge of his remaining brigades. If Chambliss's men charged, they would distract the Federals along Little's Run, permitting Hampton and Fitz Lee to pitch into their exposed and vulnerable flank. They would drive a wedge between McIntosh's line along the Low Dutch Road and the Federal artillery, and they would also encircle McIntosh's troopers and Alger's Wolverines near the Rummel farm buildings. If the plan succeeded, it would open the way to the Low Dutch Road and the rear of the Army of the Potomac. It was an excellent plan except for one thing: it did not account for the presence of the 1st Michigan and 7th Michigan cavalry regiments at the junction of the Hanover and Low Dutch roads.[1]

Captain James Breathed's battery of horse artillery was tasked with supporting the attack. Breathed brought up and deployed his guns within sight of Pennington's Federal gunners. These two batteries were familiar foes, having faced each other many times. Breathed opened and Pennington replied, both sides defiantly standing their ground.[2]

---

1 Brooke-Rawle, *Third Pennsylvania Cavalry*, 276.

2 Trout, *Galloping Thunder*, 294.

Capt. James Breathed,
commander, Breathed Battery,
Stuart Horse Artillery.

NA

As the artillery dueled, Stuart ordered the 1st Virginia Cavalry of Fitz Lee's brigade to prepare to make a mounted charge between the two Federal lines. Colonel McIntosh spotted the threat posed by the mounted column of enemy horsemen and galloped to the Lott farm buildings, where he had left the 1st Maryland Cavalry in reserve. To his chagrin, McIntosh learned that General Gregg had moved the regiment farther right to cover the intersection of the Hanover and Low Dutch roads.[3]

Major Peter Weber of the 6th Michigan likewise formed his troopers. "Men, be ready. We shall have to charge that line!"[4] Help, however, was not far away. Custer's 7th Michigan, which had been ordered to replace the 1st Maryland, was forming up to come onto the field.[5]

Lieutenant John A. Clark of the 7th Michigan was disappointed that he had not played a more active role in the fighting at Hanover on June 30. His regiment had been briefly engaged in dismounted skirmishing, but "not enough to satisfy my curiosity as the Rebs were disposed to keep at too great a distance," he wrote. "I had a curiosity to participate in a Battle and to know

3   Meyer, *Civil War Experiences*, 50-51.

4   Kidd, *Personal Recollections*, 147-148.

5   Brooke-Rawle, *Third Pennsylvania Cavalry*, 276.

Maj. Peter Weber, 6th Michigan Cavalry. Weber was killed leading a charge at Falling Waters, Maryland, on July 14, 1863.
USAHEC

what it was to charge upon the enemy." His curiosity was about to be satisfied.[6]

With the enemy attack moving in their direction, General Gregg rode to Col. William D. Mann, commander of the 7th Michigan, and ordered him to charge.[7] Custer fell in with the 7th Michigan, rode to the front, and led it across the fields. He drew his Toledo blade (emblazoned with the inscription "Draw me not without provocation. Sheathe me not without honor") and pointed it toward the enemy.[8] The 7th Michigan went from a walk to a trot, and then dashed across the fields at a gallop to meet the Virginians head-on. As the 7th Michigan neared the Confederate line, Custer wheeled in his saddle, took off his hat, and yelled, "Come on, you Wolverines!"

"There was no check to the charge," observed Capt. James H. Kidd of the 6th Michigan. "The squadrons kept in good form. Every man yelled at

6 John A. Clark to My Dear Friend, July 30, 1863, John A. Clark Papers, Bentley Historical Library, University of Michigan, Ann Arbor.

7 Mann had an interesting life. A native Ohioan, he was originally commissioned in the 1st Michigan Cavalry, and then became lieutenant colonel of the 5th Michigan. He raised and organized the 7th Michigan Cavalry and was commissioned as the new regiment's colonel in February 1863 at the young age of 23. In the years after the war, he published a scandal sheet called *Town Topics: The Journal of Society in New York City*, and was quite the rogue. He lived until 1920. For a biography, see Andy Logan, *The Man Who Robbed the Robber Barons: The Story of Colonel William d'Alton Mann: War Hero, Profiteer, Inventor, and Blackmailer Extraordinary* (New York: W. W. Norton, 1965).

8 Monahan, *Custer*, 88.

the top of his voice until the regiment had gone, perhaps, five or six hundred yards straight toward the Confederate batteries."[9] Because of a lack of ammunition, Jenkins's Southern horsemen were not there to pin them down, so the dismounted men of the 5th Michigan wheeled and opened on the flank of the charging Virginians.[10]

As the 1st Virginia advanced on the Confederate left side of the line, the two squadrons of the 3rd Pennsylvania Cavalry stationed near the Lott farmhouse raked it with volleys, forcing the Virginians to veer toward a sturdy fence running eastward from Little's Run. "A more determined and vigorous charge than was made by the First Virginia it was never my fortune to witness," confessed Capt. William E. Miller of the 3rd Pennsylvania Cavalry.[11] The Wolverines and the 1st Virginia subsequently crashed into each other at the fence, which blocked any farther advance by either regiment. "From a strong gallop to a sweeping charge around the right of the

5th we swing. The mistake is now clearly seen," observed bugler John A. Bigelow of the 5th Michigan. "But bravely the troopers ride to the death. The charge of the 'Light Brigade' was no more fiery. Officers and men all try to get over. 'Tis too bad they cannot! The rebels are too strong and too securely posted for troopers. Hand to

Col. William D'Alton Mann,
commander,
7th Michigan Cavalry.
LC

9   Kidd, *Personal Recollections*, 149.

10 John B. McIntosh to John B. Bachelder, August 27, 1885, *The Bachelder Papers*, 2:1,123.

11 Miller, "The Cavalry Battle Near Gettysburg," 404.

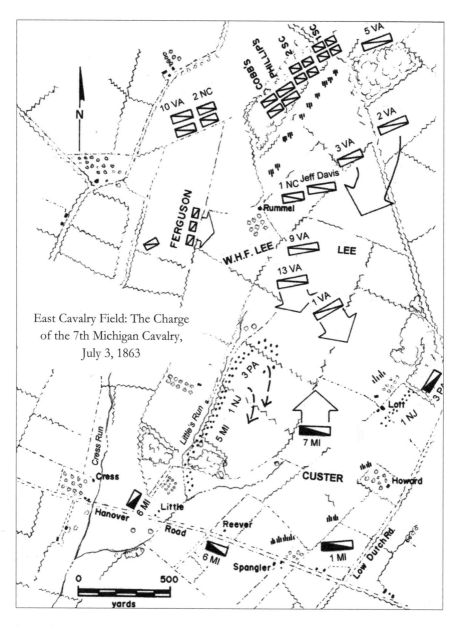

East Cavalry Field: The Charge
of the 7th Michigan Cavalry,
July 3, 1863

hand the fight is going on, on either side of the barriers. The bugle rings the
rally and the charge."[12]

12 Bigelow, "The Michigan Cavalry Brigade at Gettysburg."

"The ground over which we had to pass was very unfavorable for the maneuvering of cavalry, but despite all obstacles this regiment advanced boldly to the assault," extolled Custer in his report, "which was executed in splendid style, the enemy being driven from field to field, until our advance reached a high and unbroken fence, behind which the enemy was strongly posted. Nothing daunted, Colonel Mann, followed by the main body of his regiment, bravely rode up to the fence and discharged their revolvers in the very face of the foe."[13] As one of General Gregg's staff officers observed, "this charge was over a very considerable distance, with the result that the lines were somewhat extended so that when they came close to the enemy beyond a fence and were met by a fresh body of Confederate cavalry charging them, [they] were repulsed."[14]

Major Trowbridge watched in "astonishment and distress" as the 7th Michigan, "apparently without any attempt to change direction, dash itself upon a high staked and railed fence, squadron after squadron breaking upon the struggling mass in front, like the waves of the sea upon a rocky shore, until all were mixed in one confused and tangled mass."[15]

The trailing squadrons crashed into the mass and struggled to get over the fence. The Wolverines were "thrown into a state of indescribable confusion, though the rear troops, without order or orders, formed left and right into line along the fence, and pluckily began firing across it into the faces of the Confederates."[16] Troopers of both sides halted at the sturdy obstacle and opened fire at one another with pistols and carbines. "It was kill all you can do your best each for himself," observed Lieutenant Clark, who was now learning what it was like to see combat.[17] "Custer is a host. The men are all heroes. They stand face to face. The rebels are as brave as they. It is yelling, shooting, swearing, cutting, fight, fight-all fight. The ranks are being rapidly thinned. Horses and men are being shot down like dogs. They have us in a fix. The advantage is all on their side," observed Bigelow.[18]

---

13 Wittenberg, *At Custer's Side*, 132.

14 Meyer, *Civil War Experiences*, 50.

15 Trowbridge to Bachelder, February 19, 1886, *The Bachelder Papers*, 2:1,207.

16 Kidd, *Personal Recollections*, 149.

17 Clark to My Dear Friend, July 30, 1863.

18 Bigelow, "The Michigan Cavalry Brigade at Gettysburg."

Brig. Gen. Wade Hampton, commander, Hampton's Brigade. The South Carolina general was badly wounded at Gettysburg on July 3, 1863.

LC

"Three times the line wavered backward and forward, the honors lying first with one side and then with the other."[19]

Colonel John R. Chambliss dispatched one of his staff officers, Lt. Junius B. Jones, to find reinforcements. Jones found 45-year-old Brig. Gen. Wade Hampton, reputed to be the wealthiest man in the South, relaxing on the ground. Hampton, the son and grandson of major generals of the United States Army, had no formal military training but had proved to be a competent and popular leader of cavalry. "I liked Hampton," wrote a North Carolina horse soldier, "he waded right into them; he had dash and didn't know what fear was."[20] When Hampton heard Jones's appeal, he sprang to his feet and announced, "We must go and help" Chambliss. Hampton ordered two of his regiments, the 1st North Carolina and the Jeff Davis Legion, to charge into the sprawling combat.[21]

The raking flank fire of the 5th and 6th Michigan, the 3rd Pennsylvania, the single company of the Purnell Legion, and the 1st New Jersey blunted the Confederate charge and gave the 7th Michigan a chance to rally and reform their lines. Members of the 7th Michigan tried to tear down the stout fence

---

19 James G. Harbord, "The History of the Cavalry of the Army of Northern Virginia," quoted in Brooke-Rawle, *Third Pennsylvania Cavalry*, 318.

20 Marcus Lafayette Burnett Memoirs, Southern Historical Collection, Wilson Library, University of North Carolina, Chapel Hill, 8.

21 Statement of Lt. Junius B. Jones, *The Bachelder Papers*, 1:209-210.

Lt. George Briggs,
7th Michigan Cavalry.

*Personal Recollections of a Cavalryman
in Custer's Michigan Brigade*

blocking their way. "The task was a difficult and hazardous one, the posts and rails so firmly united that it could be accomplished only by lifting the posts, which were deeply set, and removing several lengths at once." The Wolverines finally succeeded in removing the obstacle and cleared the way. Lieutenant George Briggs of the 7th Michigan, who had three Confederate prisoners in tow, lost his horse to an enemy bullet. "With these he started to the rear, having no remount," explained Captain Kidd. "Before he could reach a place of safety, the rush of charging squadrons from either side had interrupted his retreat." Two of Briggs's prisoners escaped in the subsequent melee. The other, now determined to make Briggs his prisoner, tried to drag the lieutenant back to the Confederate lines. A stray bullet from the fight swirling around them killed the Rebel, but Briggs safely made his way back to the main Union line. He served faithfully through the rest of the war.[22]

Major James L. Carpenter led his battalion of the 7th Michigan forward in a pell-mell charge. Carpenter was near Sgt. Andrew N. Buck of Company F when Buck tried to force his way through what was left of the stout fence. A blast of enemy fire from the flank killed Buck's horse and a bullet passed through Carpenter's left side. "I felt as if someone had punched me hard with

22 Kidd, *Personal Recollections*, 150.

a stick," recalled the major, "but did not fall from my horse. I saw blood on my shirt, moved my left arm and concluded that I was not dead, then touched my horse with spurs and she jumped through the opening and passed Buck's horse." The wounded major's strength soon gave out from loss of blood, however, so he pulled his horse up short and dismounted. He let his horse go and crawled back to the fence, where he found one of his men trying to control a prisoner who looked like he was trying to escape. The major drew his revolver and threatened the man, who decided cooperation was the best option. Soon, however, Major Carpenter found himself a prisoner. "I was now tottering and looking for a safe place to lie down, when a gentlemanly Rebel asked me for my pistol. I gave it to him. He asked me if I was wounded and then said, 'Hang on to my stirrup straps and come on.'" Carpenter made it only a few yards before collapsing. His captor moved on and left the badly wounded officer behind, but Carpenter's travails were not yet over. A Pennsylvanian mistook the wounded officer for a Rebel and tried to shoot him, but his gun misfired. The Yankee horse soldier likewise turned away. After the fighting ended, Carpenter painfully crawled across the fields toward the sounds of a nearby Union camp. He called out, and the troopers—being satisfied he was not the enemy—came out to retrieve him. At the end of a long, jolting, and painful trip in an ambulance, the major received good medical care and eventually returned to his regiment.[23]

Sergeant Buck, who rode into battle next to Major Carpenter, recalled his own travails. "During this charge, while I was going through a gap in the fence I heard a ball strike my horse just back of my leg," he recounted. "Thinking he was only slightly wounded, I gave him the spur but after making one or two efforts to clear the fence he fell clear bringing one of my feet under him. I freed myself and mounted five horses in succession but found them either wounded or exhausted." When Buck learned that Major Carpenter had been severely wounded, he tried to bring him to safety, but the Confederate fire was too severe to reach him. Somhow Buck escaped injury

---

23 James L. Carpenter, "My Experience at Gettysburg," included in William O. Lee, comp., *Personal and Historical Sketches and Facial History of and by Members of the Seventh Regiment Michigan Volunteer Cavalry 1862-1865* (Detroit, MI: Ralston-Stroup Printing Co., 1904), 56-59.

and made his way back to safety when the rest of the 7th Michigan retreated.[24]

Captain James G. Birney, commander of Company D of the 7th Michigan, had his horse killed during the melee by the fence. A bullet passed through the pommel of his saddle and two more tore through his overcoat. A fourth cut through his sabre strap, and a spent ball struck him in the heel. The Wolverines were beginning to fall back when a pistol shot killed Birney's color sergeant. Birney grabbed the colors and started off to safety, but Confederate horse soldiers made for him, looking to bag both the captain and the flag. "I can assure you the bullets whistled merrily for a while, but miraculously none touched me," recalled the captain. "I shot two of the enemy, using all the charges left in my revolver and then charged a man with the pike of the colors but before I reached him I got a sabre cut on the head that laid me out." The Rebels proudly made off with the 7th Michigan's colors, and the wounded officer lay on the field for nearly an hour before the Confederates finally carried him away. Birney was held prisoner for two days, but managed to escape near Cashtown and made his way back to corps headquarters. Michigan was not able to reclaim the regiment's colors until years after the war.[25]

"No troops could have maintained this position; the Seventh was, therefore, compelled to retire, followed by twice the number of the enemy," observed General Custer. Major George K. Newcombe, who assumed command of the 7th Michigan later in the campaign, agreed: "A desperate but unequal, hand-to-hand combat here occurred."[26] A trooper of the 1st Virginia Cavalry later claimed that the men of his regiment killed 45 Yankees "in one little spot where they had to cross a fence and right together." It had indeed been a killing ground, and the Wolverines were lucky to escape from the trap along the fence.[27]

The determined counterattack by the Federals drove the Confederate troopers back past the Rummel farm buildings, where troopers from

---

24 Andrew N. Buck to his brother and sister, July 9, 1863, Michigan Historical Collections, Bentley Historical Library, University of Michigan, Ann Arbor.

25 "Extract of a Letter of Lieut. James G. Birney," included in Lee, *Seventh Regiment*, 158; "To Recover the Flag," *The National Tribune*, March 4, 1897.

26 Wittenberg, *At Custer's Side*, 126, 133.

27 Driver, *1st Virginia Cavalry*, 65-66.

Jenkins's brigade lay waiting. "Jenkins' men had nothing to do but blaze away as the blue cloud passed by them, being protected by the stone fence or wall, and they did great execution; the Yankees seemed too much occupied with their front to care about their flank. Though hundreds passed us, and but a few yards off at times, I did not see a man fire at us or even look our way," recalled one of Stuart's staff officers.[28]

Lieutenant Colonel Vincent Witcher rallied Jenkins's Virginians. "Moving my command rapidly to the left, I attacked with my dismounted men this column in flank," he recounted.[29] As Witcher's men rained severe flank fire on their exposed position along the fence, the men of the 7th Michigan broke and ran back toward their original position at the road junction.[30] A member of the 3rd Pennsylvania claimed the Wolverines "ran back like sheep."[31] Colonel McIntosh tried to rally the fleeing Michiganders, riding in their midst crying out, "For God's sake, men, if you are ever going to stand, stand now, for you are on your own free soil!" His efforts to rally the panicked horse soldiers came to naught.[32] By now, Lieutenant Clark had seen enough of real fighting to satisfy his desire to see combat. "I had my curiosity fully gratified," wrote Clark several weeks later, "& have not harkened for a fight since & do not think I should if I never participated in another."[33]

Jeb Stuart, meanwhile, realized that his attempt to reach the Hanover Road had almost succeeded with a limited attack by a fragment of his command. He concluded an all-out assault by a larger force would shatter Gregg's thin line and drive the Yankee horse soldiers from the field.[34] As General Gregg would later write of what was to come, "Severe as has been

28 Trout, *In the Saddle With Stuart*, 82.

29 Witcher to Bachelder, *The Bachelder Papers*, 2:1,238.

30 Briggs to Bachelder, 2:1,257-1,258.

31 Wert, *Gettysburg: Day Three*, 267.

32 Ibid.

33 Clark to My Dear Friend, July 30, 1863.

34 McClellan, *The Life and Campaigns of Maj. Gen. J.E.B. Stuart*, 340.

the fighting, as yet no advantage has been gained by the Rebels, & now the time has arrived for a supreme effort."[35]

The men of the 2nd Virginia Cavalry, part of Fitz Lee's brigade, advanced dismounted as sharpshooters and occupied the left of Stuart's line. In addition, Col. Thomas Owen of Lee's 3rd Virginia Cavalry, next in line to the men of the 2nd Virginia, heard the order to charge. He coolly turned to his regiment and announced, "Attention 3d Regiment, when I order you to charge I want you to follow me." Almost as of one voice, Owens's Virginians responded, "We'll do it Colonel. We'll do it." Hampton's troopers overheard this exchange and cheered the gallant Virginians. However, the order to charge was countermanded, and the 3rd Virginia did not join Stuart's grand charge.[36]

The sweeping thunderous attack was the climactic event of the large-scale cavalry battle, and it left quite an impression on the minds of the Yankee horsemen. "A grander spectacle than their advance has rarely been beheld," recalled Capt. William E. Miller of the 3rd Pennsylvania. "They marched with well-aligned fronts and steady reins. Their polished saber blades dazzled in the sun. All eyes turned upon them."[37] "In close columns of squadrons, advancing as if in review, with sabers drawn and glistening like silver in the bright sunlight—the spectacle called forth a murmur of appreciation," wrote an admiring Lt. William Brooke-Rawle.[38] Artillerist Alexander Pennington remembered it as "a beautiful sight, their guidons showing in the sunlight."[39]

The Confederate horse soldiers of Lee's remaining regiments and all of Hampton's brigade except for the Cobb Legion Cavalry steadily advanced across two farm fields toward the Lott woods, pulled down two stout rail fences to clear the way for the mounted charge, and took position behind a

35 Gregg, "Second Cavalry Division," 16.

36 Richard H. Ingram to Henry B. McClellan, April 12, 1886, *The Bachelder Papers*, 3:1,337; William R. Carter, *Sabres, Saddles, and Spurs*, Walbrook D. Swank, ed. (Shippensburg, PA: Burd Street Press, 1998), 76.

37 Miller, "The Cavalry Battle Near Gettysburg," 404.

38 Brooke-Rawle, *Third Pennsylvania Cavalry*, 277.

39 Styple, *Generals in Bronze*, 259.

fence "from which a hot fire was kept up" by the Virginians.[40] Soon, the long lines of Confederates emerged from the shelter of the woods and moved out into the open, their lines neatly dressed and their sabers glinting in the bright afternoon sun. Stuart was finally springing the jaws of his trap. "In these charges, the impetuosity of those gallant fellows, after two weeks of hard marching and hard fighting on short rations, was not only extraordinary, but irresistible," proclaimed a proud Jeb Stuart.[41]

On the Union side, David Gregg concluded, "This onset must be bravely met."[42] Captain George A. Armstrong of the 7th Michigan spurred over to Custer to point out the long lines of advancing Rebels. "Yes, I know it, and we must get back under the guns," announced Custer.[43] Captain Henry C. Meyer, one of General Gregg's staff officers, put spurs to his horse and took up a position between Pennington's and Randol's positions. Once there, he drew his saber and waited, expecting to have to help defend the guns from the Confederate charge.[44]

The Confederates rarely used their sabers, preferring instead to use pistol in close combat, so the sight of their blades at the ready made a strong impression on the Yankees. The Rebel column advanced across the farm fields, "yelling like demons," remembered one eyewitness, and reached a point about three-quarters of a mile from the Hanover Road. Pennington's and Randol's gunners opened on them there with canister.[45] Lieutenant James Chester, who commanded one of Randol's sections, fired so much

40 Carey Breckinridge to Thomas T. Munford, July 14, 1885, *The Bachelder Papers*, 2:1,112; Thomas T. Munford to John B. Bachelder, February 11, 1886, ibid., 2:1,201. The Cobb Legion had done all of the fighting at Hunterstown the day before, and had taken heavy losses. Consequently, Hampton held it out of the battle on July 3, preferring to leave the Georgians in reserve in case they were needed.

41 *OR* 27, pt. 2, 698.

42 Gregg, "Second Cavalry Division," 16.

43 George A. Armstrong, "At the Battle of Gettysburg," included in Lee, *Seventh Regiment*, 154.

44 Meyer, *Civil War Experiences*, 51.

45 James H. Kidd to his father, July 9, 1863, included in Eric J. Wittenberg, ed., *One of Custer's Wolverines: The Civil War Letters of Brevet Brigadier General James H. Kidd, 6th Michigan Cavalry* (Kent, OH: Kent State University Press, 2000), 49.

Col. Charles Town, commander of the 1st Michigan Cavalry.

Roger Hunt Collection, USAHEC

canister that replenishment had to be brought up "by the armful."[46] Their fire gouged gaps in the ranks of the Southern horse soldiers, but on they came, their rear ranks moving up and filling the gaps in the line. "Their line was almost perfect until they reached the fence that our boys had held so long," recalled a Wolverine who marveled at the precision of the advance.[47]

David Gregg realized that the moment of crisis had arrived. He had only two regiments in reserve, the 1st Michigan Cavalry and the 1st Maine Cavalry. He had little choice but to commit them to the fight or risk losing the critical crossroads. At Gregg's order, Lt. Col. Charles H. Smith, the commander of the 1st Maine, dismounted one battalion and advanced it into an orchard, while the other two battalions remained mounted in line of battle and ready to pitch in if needed. The dismounted troopers opened fire on the charging Confederates and helped to turn them back. The 1st Maine suffered one man killed—the only man killed in Gregg's division during the fighting on East Cavalry Field—plus four wounded, and one missing.[48]

Gregg dashed over to the 1st Michigan Cavalry and shouted at Col. Charles H. Town, its commander: "Colonel Town, put those people out of

---

46 James Chester to William Brooke-Rawle, September 27, 1879, *The Bachelder Papers*, 1:655.

47 Harris, *The Michigan Brigade of Cavalry*, 12-13.

48 Edward P. Tobie, "Historical Sketch," included in *Maine at Gettysburg: Report of Maine Commissioners Prepared by the Executive Committee* (Portland, ME: Lakeside Press, 1898), 497.

there."[49] Town was suffering terribly from the end stages of tuberculosis, and he was weak and frail. Even though he was dying, he had refused to leave the field. With his voice little more than a raspy whisper, Town cried, "Draw saber! Remember men; be steady, be calm, be firm! Think of Michigan! Forward—March!"[50] The 1st Michigan moved out at a trot, sabers drawn and regimental guidon snapping in the breeze. As they moved out, George Custer rode to the head of the column and said, "Colonel Town, the Seventh Cavalry has broke; I shall have to ask you to charge the Rebels."[51] The Confederates greatly outnumbered the Wolverines, but the Michigan men represented Gregg's last line of defense. "Riding at the head of the 1st Michigan was Gen. Geo. A. Custer, with drawn saber, as beautiful as the eye ever gazed upon," recalled one of Gregg's proud horsemen. "I saw the charge," remembered an admiring Pennington, "and in all I ever was in I never saw a more picturesque sight."[52]

The opposing columns gained momentum as they thundered across the open fields. "The gait increased; the charge sounded; every muscle and nerve strung to its utmost tension, every man yelling like a fiend, as the forces drew near each other."[53] The Federals could hear Southern officers

---

49 Monaghan, *Custer*, 147.

50 Bigelow, "The Michigan Cavalry Brigade at Gettysburg."

51 Many of the accounts of the fighting on East Cavalry Field (including the first edition of this book) have Custer crying out "Come on you Wolverines!" again as he led the charge of the 1st Michigan Cavalry. There is one primary source that suggests this, an account by Lt. William Brooke-Rawle of the 3rd Pennsylvania Cavalry. After examining these claims it seems highly unlikely that Brooke-Rawle could have any personal knowledge of what Custer may or may not have said since he was nowhere near the intersection of the Low Dutch and Hanover roads when the charged began. Instead, Brooke-Rawle was with Capt. William E. Miller on the flank of the Union position. Captain James H. Kidd of the 6th Michigan Cavalry stated that Custer exclaimed this when he ordered the charge of the 7th Michigan Cavalry, which makes sense. Kidd likely heard it himself. Kidd made no such claims pertaining to the charge of the 1st Michigan Cavalry, and there are no accounts of such an exclamation by Custer among the primary source accounts left by the men of the 1st Michigan Cavalry. Hence, it seems very unlikely that Custer yelled the same thing twice.

52 Harris, *The Michigan Brigade of Cavalry*, 12-13; Dewitt C. Hagadorn, "The 10th N.Y. Cav.—Porter Guard: The Great Cavalry Battle on the Right at Gettysburg," *The National Tribune*, January 25, 1906; Styple, *Generals in Bronze*, 256.

53 David M. Gilmore, "Cavalry: Its Use and Value as Illustrated by Reference to the Engagements of Kelly's Ford and Gettysburg," *Military Order of the Loyal Legion of the United States, Minnesota Commandery, Glimpses of the Nation's Series*, 2nd series, 47.

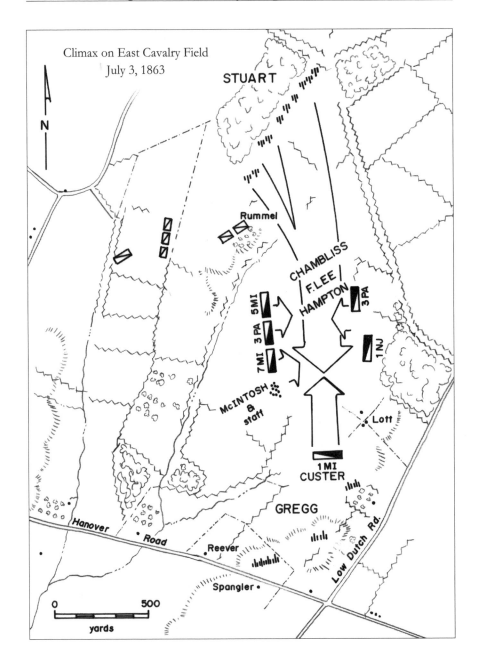

Climax on East Cavalry Field
July 3, 1863

N

STUART

Rummel

CHAMBLISS
F. LEE
HAMPTON

5 MI

3 PA

3 PA

7 MI

1 NJ

McINTOSH
&
staff

Lott

1 MI
CUSTER

GREGG

Hanover

Road

Reever

Low Dutch Rd.

Spangler

0   500
yards

encouraging their men, yelling "Keep to your sabers, men, keep to your sabers!"[54]

Seeing the opportunity to wreak havoc on the charging Confederates, dismounted Federal cavalrymen up and down the lines continued to fire on the flanks of the Southern horsemen dashing across the fields, their compact mass offering inviting targets. P. J. Malone, the 1st South Carolina Cavalry's standard bearer, received a serious wound to his side from one of the Yankee marksmen. "We had not advanced beyond two hundred yards from the cluster of trees where we had taken shelter, when I was struck, the ball entering my right side, penetrating into the abdominal cavity and lodging against or in the region of the kidneys." Malone thought he had been struck by a piece of shell fragment and tried to ignore the wound as the two sides came together. However, his right arm and side soon went numb, and he dropped his sabre and went in search of medical treatment. Malone eventually recovered from his severe wound, but his war was over.[55]

Stuart and his adjutant, Maj. Henry B. McClellan, rode out for a better view as Northern artillery shells whistled over their heads on their way to the Confederate guns blazing along Cress Ridge. The Southern gunners were doing their best, but much of their ammunition was defective and the shells detonated prematurely. When one friendly shell exploded near Stuart, an alarmed McClellan implored the Southern cavalry commander to fall back to a safer position. "Major McClellan," snapped Stuart, "you know your duty. If I fall, report to the next officer in command." Stuart remained in place, intently watching the grayclad ranks speed across the fields.[56]

Even with the poor ammunition, Breathed's artillerists stood to their hot guns. "Shell was fired as fast as men could load," noted H. H. Matthews of Breathed's battery. "The guns became so hot that I was afraid the old 2nd gun would have a premature explosion and blow No. 1 into eternity. My thumb on my left hand became burnt from thumbing the vent so that it became very painful to use it. We stayed with Pennington until dark, expending every round of ammunition." Despite the best efforts of the

---

54 Brooke-Rawle, *Third Pennsylvania Cavalry*, 278.

55 Malone, "The Charge of Black's Cavalry," 226-227.

56 Cole, *34th Battalion*, 52.

Southern gunners, Pennington's own, who had been superb all day, got the better of their old foes.[57]

Pennington was understandably proud of the role played by the Regular artillerists manning his and Randol's batteries. "The artillery—my six three-inch rifles and Randol's four Napoleons, poured a withering fire in front and fanned them out," he told sculptor James E. Kelly after the war. "Just before the [Union] charge two batteries came out on Cress's Ridge. They were put *hors de combat* by the firing of my battery alone. I kept the four guns firing simultaneously."[58]

Lieutenant Harris of the 5th Michigan was near Pennington's battery when the charge commenced. He had gone off toward Little Round Top in search of additional supplies of ammunition for his regiment and only recently had returned. Harris spurred his mount's head toward the guns, clapped both spurs to the horse's flanks, and cried out to the gunners, "Look out for the 1st Michigan!"[59]

Just then, one of Pennington's section commanders decided that things were getting a bit too hot for his comfort and decided to get out of the way. He ordered his men to limber up. Pennington heard the order and countermanded it, directing the gunners to give the Southerners a blast of double canister. "This iron hail storm was more than they could stand," recounted Harris. The Confederates veered off to the right, directly into the path of the charging 1st Michigan. "I had a beautiful view of the entire field from my position. No one had a better view than did Hamilton and I; and we could pour our fire into the Confederate cavalry until they were almost face to face with our own cavalry," recalled one of Pennington's section commanders, Lt. Carle A. Woodruff. A captured Rebel officer later told Pennington's gunners "he never saw better artillery practice and that we knocked their battery all to pieces."[60]

Earlier, when the Confederates were still nearly 1,000 yards away, Gregg had sent a staff officer over to Lt. James Chester. The staffer rode up

57 Trout, *Galloping Thunder*, 294-295.

58 Styple, *Generals in Bronze*, 256.

59 Harris, *The Michigan Brigade of Cavalry*, 15.

60 Carle A. Woodruff to James Chester, December 14, 1884, *The Bachelder Papers*, 2:1,088; Frank B. Hamilton to Carle Woodruff, November 14, 1884, *ibid.*, 2:1,078.

and said, "The General says withdraw your guns." By then it was too late for Chester, who commanded a section of Randol's battery, to withdraw his pieces, which would have led to their capture or destruction. Chester, who was "not in a cheerful humor," replied simply, "Tell the General to go to hell!"[61] Chester continued belching canister at the approaching Confederates, who came so close to Chester's section that the lieutenant could hear the Rebel officers talking to their men. The grayclad horsemen came within 75 yards of Chester's advanced pieces. As the troopers of the 1st Michigan fell back, the gunners "shouted at the top of our voice for them to divide and fall back on the flanks of our battery, but they did not heed us until they got nearly up to the muzzle of our guns, when it was almost too late for us to do anything as the enemy were upon us."[62]

Private E. A. Turner of the Jeff Davis Legion rode "through a squadron of Yankees and came very near running up to the battery. I was compelled to let my saber loose and was cut off from the regiment for some time. If the Yanks had noticed me," continued the Southern trooper, "I would have been compelled to have gone up, but they were so busily engaged that they paid no attention to me."[63]

During the entire time the Yankee gunners were under fire from Breathed's Southern horse artillerists on Cress Ridge. "The rebel shots ploughed the ground around us and the shells burst over us, but we remained steady and firm at our guns and we were finally crowned with success by completely routing the enemy and remaining in possession and victors of the field," recalled one of the Northern artillerists.[64] Chester was never censured for his refusal to obey General Gregg's orders. His heroic stand

---

61 James Chester to Carle A. Woodruff, December 29, 1884, ibid., 2:1,090. Instead of a rebuke, Chester received a brevet to captain for his service that day. So did Lt. Carle Woodruff, who commanded one of Pennington's sections. Woodruff was awarded a Medal of Honor for his valor at the July 24, 1863, battle at Newby's Crossroads in the Loudoun Valley of Virginia during the pursuit of the Army of Northern Virginia after the battle of Gettysburg. Woodruff remained in the Regular Army until 1903, retiring as a brigadier general. Heitman, *Historical Register*, 1:258, 1,097.

62 Townsend diary, 47.

63 Donald A. Hopkins, *The Little Jeff: The Jeff Davis Legion, Cavalry, Army of Northern Virginia* (Shippensburg, PA: White Mane, 1999), 157.

64 Townsend diary, 47.

demonstrated that he had correctly determined that his guns could not have been withdrawn.[65]

The charging Wolverines, meanwhile, driving north in their attack, bore down on the mass of the Southern cavalry headed directly at them. George Custer cut an impressive figure as he dashed across the open fields at the head of his troops. "His long, straight saber is gleaming in the sunshine," observed a Michigan horse soldier, "He is bareheaded and glorious. His yellow locks of hair are flying like a battle flag."[66]

The opposing forces came together with a thunderous crash. "The First Michigan struck the Rebels on their left flank, about in the middle," noted Lt. Sam Harris of the 5th Michigan, "and actually went clear through them, cutting them in two parts. The saber was all they used." The charge of the Wolverines shoved the grayclad horse soldiers aside, bunching them up so that they could not do much to defend themselves from the savage attack.[67]

During the melee, Custer's horse Roanoke went down with a minie ball to the foreleg. Custer was thrown from the injured animal, but quickly picked himself up, spotted a nearby riderless horse, and vaulted aboard. The Boy General resumed the fight, slashing at every Confederate he could reach with his sabre. He had lost his second horse in two days while leading a hell-for-leather cavalry charge.[68]

The crash of troopers, remembered Captain Miller from his vantage point in the Lott woods, was "Like the falling of timber, so sudden and violent that many of the horses were turned end over end and crushed their riders beneath them." Miller continued: "The clashing of sabers, the firing of pistols, the demands for surrender and cries of the combatants now filled the air."[69] Men on both sides remembered this point in the battle as "without doubt . . . the most gallant cavalry charge made during the war."[70] The remaining forces on the field watched the savage mounted melee unfold

65 Chester to Woodruff, *The Bachelder Papers*, 2:1,090.

66 Phipps, "Come On You Wolverines," 47.

67 Harris, *The Michigan Brigade of Cavalry*, 13.

68 George A. Custer to his sister, July 26, 1863, George A. Custer Papers, Special Collections, United States Military Academy, West Point, NY.

69 Miller, "The Cavalry Battle Near Gettysburg," 404.

70 Harris, *The Michigan Brigade of Cavalry*, 14.

before their eyes. "For many minutes the fight with sabre and pistol raged most furiously. Neither side seemed willing to give way," recalled Major McClellan, Stuart's trusted staff officer.[71]

Captain James H. Kidd of the 6th Michigan Cavalry also had an excellent view of the unfolding action. "Then it was steel to steel," he wrote after the war. "For minutes—and for minutes that seemed like years—the gray column stood and staggered before the blow; then yielded and fled. Town's impetuous charge went through it like a wedge, splitting it in twain, and scattering the Confederate horsemen."[72] "The two hostile columns tilt together, with furious clashing of sabers, intermingled with the popping of pistols," recalled a South Carolinian, "horses and riders lock together in the dread melee, friend and foe fall and are crushed beneath the angry tread. The lines of each party are swinging to and fro, backwards and forwards."[73]

Major William A. Morgan of the 1st Virginia Cavalry, a 32-year-old farmer from Jefferson County in what is now West Virginia, left an especially vivid description of the raging melee:

> The fighting now became furious. Charge after charge was here given and received. Each party reformed only to charge again. Prisoners were taken and retaken in a very few moments, as the surging men of either side would crash through the line, only to be decimated and hurled back. The fighting became hand-to-hand, blow for blow, cut for cut, and oath for oath. It seemed as if the very furies from the infernal regions were turned loose on each other. For some time this fighting continued along our entire line with unusual fury. The artillery on both sides were at close range, handled with energy, and were terribly destructive. The entire plain was thickly strewn with wounded and dead men and horses. Gradually, as if satiated, the lines drifted apart, the mounted regiments being replaced by dismounted skirmishers.[74]

---

71 McClellan, *The Life and Campaigns of Maj. Gen. J.E.B. Stuart*, 340.

72 Kidd, *Personal Recollections*, 155.

73 Ulysses R. Brooks, *Stories of the Confederacy* (Columbia, SC: The State Co., 1912), 176.

74 Bruce S. Allardice, *Confederate Colonels: A Biographical Register* (Columbia: University of Missouri Press, 2008), 282; Morgan, "Desperate Charges."

The Charge at Gettysburg.
Battles and Leaders

"We advanced at the charge with drawn sabers as the enemy did the same toward us," recalled a Virginian. "We met near the center of that field where sabre met sabre and pistol shots followed in quick succession. Because we tried to ride the enemy down, the individual encounters were often decided by the weight and strength of the animals. The battle grew hotter and hotter, horses and men were overthrown or shot and many were killed and wounded."[75] Another Virginian recalled that "the field is soon alive with moving squadrons here a group retiring in disorder—there a mass mixed up in hand to hand conflict; horses rearing, swords uplifted, smoke and dust."[76] Breathed's gunners had a bird's eye view of the scene unfolding in front of them. "For many minutes the fight raged, pistol and saber being used freely," recounted one of the artillerists. "Neither force seemed willing to give way and held tenaciously like two bulldogs."[77]

As they mixed promiscuously, men of both sides hacked and slashed at each other in the middle of the field, and savage individual combat raged all around. It made for a terrible but compelling sight. "Horses were knocked down like pins, stunned, and some killed outright," recounted Dr. Theodore Tate of the 3rd Pennsylvania Cavalry. "Thus riders were unhorsed, and men and horses were struggling and fighting still." A nameless dismounted Rebel "ran his sabre up the entire back of a Union cavalryman as he sat on his horse, the point of the blade coming out at the shoulder; fortunately, it was only a flesh wound, but the course and force of the saber thrust showed the blind fury of the intention that impelled it."[78]

The force of the collision knocked men from the saddle, leaving the dismounted troopers to fend for themselves amidst struggling beasts and thundering hooves. "Men pitched themselves out of their saddles, and, by the force of the momentum, hurled themselves head foremost, like battering rams, at each other. These men were simply struggling to kill, with no thought of self or saving or protecting themselves—eager to die, even if they

---

75 Garland C. Hudgins and Richard B. Kleese, eds., *Recollections of an Old Dominion Dragoon: The Civil War Experiences of Sgt. Robert S. Hudgins II, Co. B, 3rd Virginia Cavalry* (Orange, VA: Publisher's Press, 1993), 82-84.

76 Stephens Calhoun Smith, "Personal Reminiscences of Gettysburg," Gettysburg National Military Park, Gettysburg, PA, 2 (GNMP).

77 Trout, *Memoirs of the Stuart Horse Artillery Battalion*, vol. 2, 99.

78 *1886 History of Adams County Pennsylvania* (Chicago: Warner, Beers Co., 1886), 172.

could kill the enemy and take him with them over the bank, and into the dark, deep pit where dwelt death and silence."[79]

One of the Wolverines bore down on S. S. Murrill, a member of the 2nd Virginia Cavalry. Murrill shot him, "and his horse left him, so as I only had 3 cartridges left from 42 that morning, my first impulse was to get cartridges, I rolled him over & found an army pistol, which I took, but the cartridges were for a Burnside [carbine] so I could not use them in a Sharp's rifle." Three Yankee horse soldiers targeted Murrill, ordering him to surrender. Murrill "declined by giving them one of the three Sharp's cartridges I had left. Then the other two feeling sure of their prize charged upon me & ordered my surrender, in answer to which I drew the captured pistol & fired & they hurried away." A relieved Murrill made it safely back to the main Southern line of battle along Cress Ridge.[80]

A big redheaded Confederate officer tried to rally his men, twirling his sabre. "Come on you cowards," he cried, "will you stop for a hand full of Yanks?" Lieutenant Peter Karpp of the 1st Michigan dashed up to the grayclad officer, his own sabre flashing, and "sooner than it takes to write it, the officer sinks to the ground under Karpp's terrific blow."[81]

Private Thomas Shephard of the 1st Michigan Cavalry carried the regiment's headquarters flag into battle that afternoon. When Southern horsemen surrounded him, Shephard tore the colors from its staff and tucked them into his tunic to carry the flag safely into captivity. The unfortunate Shephard spent 505 days in Confederate prisons, but somehow managed to keep the flag safely the whole time. He returned it home to Michigan intact at the end of the war.[82]

Stephens Calhoun Smith of the 5th Virginia Cavalry rode into battle that day on a big beautiful horse liberated from a Pennsylvania farmer. The horse carried him to the head of the charging column, and "in a few minutes I was completely surrounded," he recalled. "I discharged every barrel of my pistol and then went to work with my sabre, I brought it out bathed in blood. How I

---

79 Ibid.

80 S. S. Murrill to Thomas T. Munford, May 8, 1886, *The Bachelder Papers*, 3:1,378-1,379.

81 C. M. Norton to Amasa E. Matthews, July 3, 1886, ibid., 3:1,436.

82 "How Another Flag Went Through," *The National Tribune*, April 13, 1892.

escaped is wonderful as I had many shots fired at me within a few feet of my head. In going into the fight I placed my trust in God and I feel that his hand protected me and brought me safely through."[83]

Caught up in the grandeur of the event, Fitz Lee had impetuously pitched into the magnificent charge at the head of his brigade. The short and stout brigadier engaged in a saber duel with an "athletic" Federal officer who proved his equal as a swordsman. The Yankee seemed to be getting the better of the duel, and Fitz was enough of a warrior to know he was in trouble. So did his comrades witnessing the struggle. "I had given him up as lost," remembered an officer of the 2nd Virginia Cavalry, "as they were close on him."[84] Lee's adjutant, Maj. James D. Ferguson, dashed up and saved the general with a quick and well-aimed pistol shot that felled the Northerner just as he was "making the confident thrust at him." Fitz Lee wisely withdrew to the safety of Cress Ridge, where he watched his brigade tangle with the Federal horsemen.[85]

Captain Amasa E. Matthews, whose squadron of the 1st Michigan brought up the rear of the charge of the Wolverines, found it difficult to maintain discipline in the raging fight. "I never worked harder in my life than behind this column to keep the wild furious men from using their pistols, shooting themselves, and breaking up the ranks," he recalled. "I thought we was doing the best, so long as the sabre points kept them running, it was good enough, but knowing full well they would sometime come when we would let up, I expected all hands would pitch in and carry back a rebel or two on each sabre." Matthews watched as several Wolverines wavered and turned back, but he stopped them, admonishing them to "follow the retreating Confederates." His men kept to the sabre "while the enemy dashed backwards and forward, shooting in [their] faces" until they "struck a gap that caused the 'jam.'" The "frenzied Confederates drove so forcibly" and their losses were so great that Captain Matthews decided "prudence and discretion dictated a hasty retreat." He retired to the woods along the Union

83 Stephen Calhoun Smith to his parents, July 12, 1863, copy in files, Gettysburg National Military Park.

84 Edward Brugh to Thomas T. Munford, April 27, 1886, Brake Collection.

85 D. B. Rea, *Sketches of Hampton's Cavalry, Embracing the Principal Exploits of the Cavalry in the Campaigns of 1862 and 1863* (Columbia, SC: South Carolinian Steam Press, 1864), 116.

right and watched as Capt. George W. Alexander's Second Squadron struck the Confederates that had pursued him.[86]

An opportunity for a counterattack had arrived. The Federal line along Little's Run turned about from the Rummel farm and raked the Confederate right flank with volley after volley. On Colonel Alger's orders, Maj. Luther S. Trowbridge of the 5th Michigan told his men to mount up and join the charge. The Wolverines dashed to their horses and joined the attack, crashing into the right flank of Fitz Lee's charging column. "The charge was not made in very good order, it was in such haste that the men had not time to form," admitted Trowbridge after the battle, "yet it had the desired effect and started the enemy in wild confusion over the field." Before long the major's horse was shot out from under him. "Then I was half a mile nearly from the balance of my regt—my horse killed—the rebs all around me so here's for Richmond thought I."[87] Billy Dunn, Trowbridge's orderly, gave the major his horse and was promptly captured for his trouble. Fortunately, Dunn escaped and made his way back to his regiment just before dark. Because the charge had now passed them by, and with the melee raging, Trowbridge's men fell back. While Trowbridge's battalion retired, the 1st Virginia charged into its flank. In turn, Col. Russell Alger led his battalion in a determined countercharge that drove back the Virginians, enabling Trowbridge's men to reach safety.[88]

"It was while in this line of battle that I came very near getting a call," recalled Sgt. Henry Avery of the 5th Michigan. "I noticed a cannon smoke in front, and a little to the left; the ball came past my horse's head, brushed my knee, and struck the man beside me, tearing his leg and passing through his horse, rolling them together on the ground."[89]

Seeing the Confederate charge bearing down on them, Lt. Daniel Littlefield's squadron of the 7th Michigan rallied and joined the charge of the 1st Michigan, adding their weight to the Union attack. Likewise, the Purnell Legionnaires, swept aside by the grand Confederate charge, resumed

---

86 Amasa E. Matthews to John B. Bachelder, June 11, 1887, *The Bachelder Papers*, 3:1,492.

87 Trowbridge letter.

88 Kidd, *Personal Recollections*, 152.

89 Husby and Wittenberg, *Under Custer's Command*, 37.

Capt. Walter Newhall, 3rd Pennsylvania Cavalry, was badly wounded on East Cavalry Field.

History of the Third Pennsylvania Cavalry in the American Civil War of 1861-1865

their former position on the Rebel right flank, where they raked the enemy and drove the charging grayclad horsemen toward the belching Union horse artillerists, whose guns tore great holes in their ranks.[90]

It was about this time that Colonel McIntosh dispatched his adjutant, Capt. Walter S. Newhall of the 3rd Pennsylvania Cavalry, to the left end of the Little's Run line with orders for Capts. Charles Treichel and William W. Rogers. They held a position squarely on the Rebel right flank, but because the Pennsylvanians there occupied a little valley, they were hidden from the charging Rebels. McIntosh ordered Treichel and Rogers to mount as many men as possible and ride into the head of the Confederate column. After briefly explaining his orders to the small party, staffer Newhall drew his saber and led the charge as just sixteen enlisted men and five officers of the 3rd Pennsylvania crashed into the color guard of Hampton's regiments.[91] Newhall, "sharing the excitement of the moment," led the dash. He grabbed for Hampton's

90 Gibson, "Address of Captain William Gibson," 105.

91 Sally Butler Wister, *Walter S. Newhall: A Memoir* (Philadelphia: The Sanitary Commission, 1864), 111.

Capt. Charles Treichel,
commander of a squadron of the
3rd Pennsylvania Cavalry.

*History of the Third Pennsylvania Cavalry in the
American Civil War of 1861-1865*

guidon, but "a sabre cut was directed at his head, and he was compelled to parry it." The color bearer, William A. Harrison, lowered his staff, and using it like a lance, "struck Newhall full tilt in the face, knocking him senseless on the ground." Newhall was wounded by both a pistol shot and a sabre cut to the face in his fight for the colors.[92]

When Newhall recovered consciousness, he discovered he lay between the two lines, with artillery shells occasionally bursting around him. His wounds bled profusely, he had lost his weapons, and he had been left for dead. When the injured captain found he had strength enough to walk, he hobbled his way to the safety of the Union lines. He informed Lieutenant Chester what had happened and asked him to "tell the General of his mishap, and explain his absence from the field."[93] As Newhall staggered off in search of medical assistance, he realized he had come "in at a point where there was some slight confusion under a very heavy fire, [and] rallied the men, who were becoming unsteady, and then made the best of his way to find a surgeon." There, he found his lifelong friend Captain Treichel. He had lost his horse, been wounded in the arm by a Confederate ball, captured, and then eventually escaped. Later in the day, Newhall's brothers, who were also officers, found the two injured men lying in a nearby farmhouse among other wounded. "Walter was

92 Brooke-Rawle, *Third Pennsylvania Cavalry*, 258.

93 James Chester to John B. Bachelder, November 27, 1884, *The Bachelder Papers*, 2:1,280.

exceedingly lame and bruised, in consequence of the fall from his horse, and his wound was so stiff and swollen that he had the greatest difficulty in articulating, but he was in high spirits over the victory."[94]

"Our brave Walt was wounded yesterday, painfully but not dangerously," recounted Newhall's brother, Capt. Frederick C. Newhall of the 6th Pennsylvania Cavalry, who served as one of Pleasonton's staff officers. "He was shot in the chin by a pistol ball which passed out along his cheek." Frederick also noted, "Charley Treichel is shot in the fleshy part of the arm, not at all serious. His horse was killed being shot in five places. Their conduct there is said by everybody there to be perfectly superb." Captain Rogers was also seriously wounded twice in the chest during this headlong charge.[95]

Sergeant Joe Rammel of Company B of the 3rd Pennsylvania charged that day with his comrades and forced his way into the ranks of the Rebel horsemen. A huge Rebel raised his sabre to deliver a "front cut." Rammel parried the blow with the center of his sabre blade, which caused the Confederate's blade to slide down to the guard, crushed it, and laid open the sergeant's finger to the bone. Rammel spurred forward and gripped his saddle tightly with his knees, "the left one striking that of his opponent, who had raised in his stirrups to deliver the stroke." The force of the blow knocked the big Rebel from his horse, permitting Rammel to pass to safety without further injury. Rammel's horse had broken his curb chain and "consequently it was difficult to manage, but he headed him for our line and rolled his spurs into him until he got safely back out of the melee and repaired the curb chain." Rammel kept that sabre as a treasured souvenir of the day's combat, even though it was useless for further fighting.[96]

Colonel McIntosh gathered his staff officers, headquarters' escort, and any other miscellaneous men who could be found, "consulted my officers as to the propriety of a charge, and they agreed that an effort was demanded of

94 "In Memoriam Charles Treichel," *The Cavalry Society of the United States* (Concord, NH: published by the Society, 1894), 281. Captain Newhall survived his bad wound only to drown in the Rappahannock River in December of 1863. Wister, *Walter S. Newhall*, 112-113.

95 Frederick C. Newhall to Thomas Newhall, July 4, 1863, Newhall family papers, Historical Society of Pennsylvania; Brooke-Rawle, *Third Pennsylvania Cavalry*, 258, 279.

96 Ibid., 304.

Capt. William E. Miller,
commander of Co. H,
3rd Pennsylvania Cavalry.
USAHEC

us." McIntosh and his brave little band charged into the right front of the Rebel column.[97] Minutes dragged by like hours as the two sides fought "amid the clashing of the sabers, the rattle of the small arms, the frenzied imprecations, the demands to surrender, the undaunted replies and the appeals for mercy, the Confederate column [standing] its ground."[98] Staff officers, orderlies, and men who just a moment before had been headed for the rear turned about and pitched into the melee raging in front of the Federal guns.[99] Although the charge by McIntosh and these elements of the 3rd Pennsylvania was over quickly, their contribution helped break up the Confederate charge and blunt its effect.

Meanwhile, on the opposite end of the Confederate line, more danger awaited the charging Southerners from an unexpected direction. When the day started, Capt. William E. Miller was plagued by a terrible cramp. The 27-year-old was a native of nearby Cumberland County, Pennsylvania. He had enlisted in Company H of the 3rd Pennsylvania Cavalry as a private in August 1861, and was commissioned first lieutenant when the regiment was organized that fall. At the September 1862 battle of Antietam, Lieutenant Miller drew the first fire of the Army of Northern Virginia during that bloody battle after Maj. Gen. Joseph Hooker's First Corps advance across Antietam Creek. For his valor that day, Miller was promoted to captain and

---

97 McIntosh to Bachelder, *The Bachelder Papers*, 1:653.

98 Brooke-Rawle, *Third Pennsylvania Cavalry*, 279-280.

99 Meyer, *Civil War Experiences*, 52.

command of Company H, bypassing other more senior lieutenants. He had served bravely and honorably in all of the campaigns of the 3rd Pennsylvania Cavalry to date, and was well-regarded by his whole regiment.[100]

Unwilling to miss any action, Miller asked his friend Capt. David M. Gilmore to rub out the cramp. Using whiskey, Gilmore was massaging it when orders to mount arrived, "jerking the cramp out of me," recalled Miller.[101] His orders were to hold his position in the Lott woods at all hazards. "He was almost adored by the men of his company, and they would follow him anywhere, and do anything he ordered them to do," recalled Lt. William Brooke-Rawle. "A brave soldier, a gallant officer, as reliable a cavalry commander as ever drew a sabre or threw his leg over a horse, a true man, one to count on every time, his word would be taken by any officer or man in the regiment."[102]

Miller's squadron was stretched along the edge of the Lott farm woodlot on the Confederate left flank several hundred yards directly across the field from the position held by Treichel's and Newhall's men. Miller's men had a clear view of the charging Confederates, but they were hidden by a swale—and the Southern horsemen had no idea the Pennsylvanians were there. The Confederate line paralleled Miller's several hundred yards away.[103]

As the action unfolded in front of him, Miller realized that his men could make a difference in the outcome of the fight. The Confederate grand charge was gathering momentum when the left flank of Hampton's and Fitz Lee's troopers passed directly in front of Miller's position. "Lieutenant [Brooke-Rawle] of my squadron stood on a knoll in front of my command where we had an elegant view of all that was going on," wrote the captain in a letter to his brother. "We soon discovered that Stuart was too heavy for Custer, and unless some diversion was made all would be lost." Miller

100 Charles Hanna, *Gettysburg Medal of Honor Recipients* (Springville, UT: Bonneville Books, 2010), 197-198.

101 Brooke-Rawle, *Third Pennsylvania Cavalry*, 306.

102 William Brooke Rawle, "A Refutation by William Brooke-Rawle" William Brooke-Rawle Papers, Historical Society of Pennsylvania, Philadelphia, 9.

103 Andrew J. Speese, *Story of Companies H, A and C, Third Pennsylvania Cavalry at Gettysburg, July 3, 1863* (Philadelphia: privately published, 1907), 8.

Lt. William Brooke-Rawle, Co. H,
3rd Pennsylvania Cavalry. He
would become one of the leading
historians of the fighting on
East Cavalry Field.

*History of the Third Pennsylvania Cavalry in the
American Civil War of 1861-1865*

turned to his executive officer,
Brooke-Rawle, and announced,
"I have been ordered to hold this
position, but if you will back me
up in case I am court-martialed
for disobedience, I will order a
charge."[104]

Brooke-Rawle voiced his
agreement, and Miller gave his orders. His mounted command fired a volley
and then, shouting to his men to draw their sabers, he led them in a pell-mell
mounted charge that pierced the Confederate column, cutting off nearly
one-third of it and driving the fragment back toward Cress Ridge. "Miller
swept like a thunderbolt from the right and struck the column about the
middle and cut his way clear through, cutting off a portion and driving it
back as far as Rummel's barn, although himself wounded."[105] Miller's
impetuous charge passed all the way through the Confederates, almost to the
Little's Run line, which blazed with carbine fire. A fence line along the run
forced Miller's men to the right, where they came under flanking fire from

---

104 William E. Miller to his brother, July 7, 1863, William Brooke-Rawle Papers,
Historical Society of Pennsylvania, Philadelphia; Miller, "The Cavalry Battle Near
Gettysburg," 404-405. Corporal Andrew J. Speese of Miller's Company H vigorously
disputed the claims of Miller and Brooke-Rawle that Miller ordered the charge. According
to Speese, Miller's men made the charge spontaneously, without his ordering it. Speese was
so vehement in his insistence that Miller had not ordered the charge that he wrote and
published a pamphlet to refute the claim.

105 Statement of Capt. David M. Gilmore, included in William E. Miller Medal of Honor
file, RG 94, Entry No. 496, Box 1391.

Captain Miller's Charge.

Deeds of Valor

the Southerners along the run and from the Confederate artillery in the distance.[106] "Breathed's battery, unsupported, was only one hundred yards away, but my men were so disabled and scattered that they were unable to take it," recalled a disappointed Miller.[107]

At the entrance to the Rummel wagon shed, a Confederate trooper slashed at Miller so violently it snapped the captain's sabre in two. Miller threw away the hilt, covered the Rebel with his pistol, and captured the man. Miller took a moment to reform his line before his squadron cut its way back through the Confederates a second time, cutting off a portion of Fitz Lee's

106 Speese, *The Story of Companies H, A and C*, 12. In 1907, Speese wrote, "No small body of men, however brave, could have pierced that solid mass of sturdy Confederates, even if the fence had not been a barrier. This fence deflected the men in blue to the right towards Rummel's spring house, and only a small number got in the rear of the Confederates through the fence at places where the rails had been thrown down. It was a sheer, and utter, an absolute impossibility to cut the column in two by the physical force at hand, even if the men had been in column and competently officered." Ibid.

107 Miller, "The Cavalry Battle Near Gettysburg," 404-405.

Cpl. Andrew J. Speese, Co. H,
3rd Pennsylvania Cavalry.
Speese made the charge with
Capt. William E. Miller at the
climax of the fighting on
East Cavalry Field.

*History of the Third Pennsylvania Cavalry in the
American Civil War of 1861-1865*

brigade before reaching the safety of the Lott woods once more.[108] Remarkably, Miller suffered only a scratch on his right arm. Instead of a court martial, and with David Gregg's ringing endorsement, Miller received a Medal of Honor years after the war. Fourteen years later, while visiting John Rummel, Miller found his saber hilt and a portion of the blade among the relics collected by Rummel after the battle.[109]

During the mounted charge, Lt. Brooke-Rawle reached for his revolver, which he had tucked into his boot. He drew the weapon and tried to cock it, but the hammer wouldn't budge. Frustrated, the lieutenant hurled the pistol "into the face of a rebel who in perfervid language, was doing his best to persuade [Brooke-Rawle] to accompany him as a prisoner." Fortunately, Brooke-Rawle's tactic startled the Confederate horseman, and the lieutenant rejoined his squadron as it cut its swath back through the enemy cavalry.[110]

---

108 Ibid.; Brooke-Rawle, *Third Pennsylvania Cavalry*, 279.

109 Captain Miller's Medal of Honor citation reads: "At Gettysburg, Pa., July 3, 1863, this officer, then Captain 3d Pennsylvania Cavalry, and commanding a squadron of four troops of his regiment, seeing an opportunity to strike in flank an attacking column of the enemy's cavalry, that was then being charged in front, exceeded his instructions and without orders led a charge of his squadron upon the flank of the enemy, checked his attack, cut off and dispersed the rear of his column."

110 Brooke-Rawle, "A Refutation," 31.

Corporal Andrew J. Speese of Miller's Company H remembered the bravery of one particular Confederate color bearer. "Riding in the rear on a gray horse, he waved the flag and defied the Yankees to take it," he recalled years later. "We tried hard to snipe him and secure the colors, but without success. After these Confederates reached Rummel's lane, they formed in the field beyond, about 200 yards in front of their battery. Seeing our weakness, and that their guns were in no danger from us, they in turn advanced and we were forced to retreat." Speese could not remember seeing any of the Keystone State men reach the Rummel fields.[111]

The many spontaneous small unit actions, such as Captain Miller's charge, showed that the Federal horsemen had learned to take the initiative and act on their own instincts. These flanking attacks and the severe flanking fire of the Northern gunners did much to take the steam out of the rolling Confederate juggernaut. When Miller's charge crashed into their flank, the surprised Virginians of Fitz Lee's brigade believed that a much larger force had hit them—and many broke and ran. The experience and training of these Northern horse soldiers paid dividends that long afternoon, and General Gregg had every right to be proud of their performance.

Colonel McIntosh had earlier sent one of his staff officers, Capt. Hampton S. Thomas of the 1st Pennsylvania Cavalry, to clear the route of the 1st Michigan of dismounted skirmishers. After doing so, he rode to the Lott springhouse, dismounted, and sat on a fence to watch the subsequent action. Thomas asked a trooper of the 1st New Jersey if the water could be drunk, and was dipping a cool drink when an enemy bullet whizzed by his head. The Confederate "was standing at the corner of a shed. Before he could reload, I jumped over the spring, frog-fashion, and rolled around behind the spring house." Thomas found Capt. James H. Hart's squadron of the 1st New Jersey restlessly waiting for orders along the Low Dutch Road. Thomas knew the 3rd Pennsylvania needed help, so he implored the squadron to join in. The Jerseymen agreed, and drove off the Confederates near the Lott house before pitching into the fighting in front of them. "In the melee, near the colors, was an officer of high rank, and the two headed the squadron for that part of the fight." The Jerseymen drew sabers and charged into the Confederate left flank just south of Miller's charge. Several of the New Jersey troopers closed

---

111 Speese, *Story of Companies H, A and C*, 9.

in on Wade Hampton and engaged him in a sword duel in the battle's final compelling drama.[112]

Hampton had not expected to lead a charge that day. After riding to find Stuart, he was shocked to spot his brigade in motion, having been ordered to charge by Fitz Lee. Hampton countermanded the order, "as I did not think it a judicious one, and the brigade resumed its former position." A few minutes later, Colonel Chambliss rode up to Hampton and reported that he had been sent to ask Lee for support, but Lee told him that Hampton's brigade was closer. Lee instructed Chambliss to ask the South Carolinian for troops. Recognizing that support was essential, Hampton sent Col. Laurence S. Baker's 1st North Carolina Cavalry and Lt. Col. J. Fred Waring's Jeff Davis Legion to support Chambliss, and then "rode rapidly to the front to take charge of these two regiments, and, while doing this, to my surprise saw the rest of my brigade (except the Cobb Legion) and Fitz Lee's Brigade charging." Hampton, who was not the sort to shrink from combat, spurred ahead, his long broadsword waving in the bright afternoon sun.[113]

Mounted on Butler, his favorite charger, the big South Carolinian cried, "Charge them, my brave boys, charge them!" as he led his brigade forward at the gallop. Charging without making any preparations to tear down fences, and forced to use a narrow lane, his column suffered a raking fire from the Union gunners. Hampton's men raised their sabers with a wild Rebel yell as they prepared to crash into their foemen.[114]

Hampton's brigade flag, fluttering in front, led the Southern advance. "It was the moment for which cavalry wait all their lives—the opportunity which seldom comes—that vanishes like shadows on glass," observed one poetically inclined Confederate. "If the Federal cavalry were to be swept from their place on the right, the road to the rear of their center gained, now was the time."[115] The color bearer of the 1st South Carolina Cavalry rode alongside Hampton as the battle line moved out. "We started out in fine style, and one continued shout arose from the charging column," he recalled.

---

112 Hampton S. Thomas to John B. Bachelder, July 1, 1886, *The Bachelder Papers*, 3:1,432; Brooke-Rawle, *Third Pennsylvania Cavalry*, 280.

113 *OR* 27, pt. 2, 724-725.

114 Rea, *Sketches from Hampton's Cavalry*, 116.

115 Harbord, "The History of the Cavalry," quoted in Brooke-Rawle, *Third Pennsylvania Cavalry*, 319.

"Hampton's Cavalry Fight at Gettysburg." *John Esten Cooke's Wearing of the Gray; Being Personal Portraits, Scenes and Adventures of the War*

"The intervening ground over which we were passing was so crossed and seamed with fences and ditches as to greatly impede our progress."[116]

And then the impact occurred. "The two hostile columns tilt together, with furious clashing of sabers, intermingled with the popping of pistols; horses and riders lock together in the dread melee, friend and foe fall and are crushed beneath the angry tread," remembered one of Hampton's troopers. "The lines of each party are swinging to and fro, backwards and forwards, finally enemy's begin to waver, and are being thrust back slowly at the point of the saber," when the charging 1st Michigan came up.[117]

One of Chambliss' Virginians watched Hampton lead his command into battle. "[The Rummel] barn was a conspicuous mark" to the Federals, who threatened to "capture the whole body of dismounted men when Hampton came into view at the head of his column," he wrote. "For a time as he dashed toward the barn he held the colors in his right hand, and the men responded to his intrepid action with a mighty yell. Just as he closed in on the foe he passed the flag back to its bearer at his side, and the bloody work began."[118]

The shock of Hampton's charge was immediate and shattered the 1st Michigan's position. "We huddled together and the [enemy] was pouring a destructive fire among us. No wonder that we ran," observed a Wolverine.[119] The heavy force of Confederate horsemen drove the 1st Michigan away from the fence (as earlier described), and the grayclad troopers crossed the wall and pressed the Wolverines back toward the Hanover Road.[120]

Hampton had ridden over to try to extricate the 1st North Carolina and the Jeff Davis Legion when he drew the attention of several Federals. Hemmed in against a fence, he cut one down with his broadsword and another with his pistol. Two Mississippians of the Jeff Davis Legion, Pvts. Jordan Moore and John Dunlap, tried to rescue the brigade commander, but were cut from their saddles by Yankee sabers. Another attacker fell to

---

116 P. J. Malone, "Charge of Black's Cavalry Regiment at Gettysburg," *Southern Historical Society Papers*, vol. 16 (1888), 225.

117 Rea, *Sketches from Hampton's Cavalry*, 116.

118 George W. Beale, "General Wade Hampton: Tribute from a Virginian Who Served Under Him," *Richmond Dispatch*, May 4, 1902.

119 Longacre, *Custer and His Wolverines*, 150.

120 George G. Briggs to John B. Bachelder, March 26, 1886, *The Bachelder Papers*, 2:1,257.

Hampton's pistol as he fought on alone. One Federal cut Hampton's scalp with his saber before a second Yankee rode up behind Hampton and shot him in the side. "While he parried manfully the blows being rained on his devoted head," recorded a Georgian of Cobb's Legion, "he turned his head with those snapping eyes flashing upon the man who shot him and said, 'You dastardly coward—shoot a man from the rear!'"[121]

Blood soaked and with his vision blurred, Hampton rode to the aid of another Southern trooper. The general fenced with a Yankee, who scored with another stroke to Hampton's head. An enraged Hampton raised his heavy sword down high in the air, then swept it down on the Yankee's head with all his considerable strength and cleft his adversary's skull all the way down to the chin. Northern troopers surged toward the injured South Carolinian and pinned him against the fence. His capture or death seemed inevitable, but Hampton fought on. Fortunately, some of his men spotted their commander's predicament and galloped to his aid. Sergeant Nat Price of the 1st North Carolina killed a man who aimed a blow at the general's head. Along with a Georgian of the Cobb Legion, Price succeeded in opening a narrow corridor for Hampton's escape. "General, general, they are too many for us," cried a frantic Price. "For God's sake, leap your horse over the fence; I'll die before they have you." As the Federals formed to charge him again, Hampton spurred his horse Butler and soared over the fence to safety as Sergeant Price shot the nearest of the enemy and leaped to safety just behind his injured general. Covered with blood and badly wounded, Hampton somehow made it off the field. "Ten minutes before I had conversed with the noble South Carolinian, and he was full of life, strength and animation," recalled one of Stuart's staff officers. "Now he was slowly being borne to the rear in his ambulance, bleeding from his dangerous wounds."[122]

As he was being carried from the field, Hampton called for Col. Laurence S. Baker of the 1st North Carolina Cavalry, the ranking colonel of his brigade, to take command. The wounded brigadier encouraged his men

---

121 Wiley C. Howard, *Sketches of Cobb Legion Cavalry and Some Incidents and Scenes Remembered* (privately published, 1901), 8-9.

122 Brooks, *Stories of the Confederacy*, 175-177; John Esten Cooke, *Wearing of the Gray; Being Personal Portraits, Scenes and Adventures of the War* (New York: E.B. Treat & Co., 1867), 247.

to fight on and not give up the field. "They [caught] the inspiration from the wounded hero, together with the encouragement of the gallant officer at their head, and turn[ed] upon the pressing foe with a new energy," recounted one of Hampton's admiring troopers. "Gen. Hampton was severely wounded— two saber cuts on the head and shot in the thigh," reported an officer from Georgia. "His wounds are thought to be not dangerous but painful and severe." Hampton's fractured skull and wounded side would take time to heal. The general would not be well enough to resume command of his brigade until later that fall. Baker remained at the helm of Hampton's brigade until the general resumed his duties in September.[123]

As this part of the fight was swirling in deadly combat, Pvt. J. G. McReynolds of the Phillips Legion Cavalry dashed straight for the belching Union guns. "Like some demon phantom," McReynolds called out, "Come on, boys, come on! My God, let's take the battery!" When McReynolds looked back, however, his comrades were retiring. He wisely put spurs to horse and galloped back, dodging missiles big and small as he went.[124]

The colors of the Jeff Davis Legion of Hampton's brigade were nearly captured three different times during the melee. "It fell three times under the hot fire but never reached the ground as quick and ready hands caught it as either color bearer or his mount went down," recalled trooper George N. Saussy of Company F of the Jeff Davis Legion 50 years after the Civil War.[125]

Having been hit on three sides, and with Yankees in their front and with other Yankee forces of unknown strength operating on both flanks, the Confederate charge lost its momentum. The Southerners were unable to reach the Union batteries before they were forced to retreat back toward the Rummel farm buildings, all the way to Cress Ridge and the woods beyond the barn. They pulled back to the north of the Rummel barn and formed a thin skirmish line and left the rest of the field in the hands of the victorious Yankee troopers who had swept them away. "For a moment, but only a moment, that long, heavy column stood its ground; then, unable to withstand the impetuosity of our attack, it gave way in a disorderly rout, leaving vast

---

123 Rea, *Sketches from Hampton's Cavalry*, 117; William G. Delony to his wife, July 4, 1863, copy in files, Gettysburg National Military Park.

124 Rea, *Sketches from Hampton's Cavalry*, 118.

125 Hopkins, *The Little Jeff*, 157.

numbers of dead and wounded in our possession" boasted Custer, "while the First, being masters of the field, had the proud satisfaction of seeing the much vaunted chivalry, led by their favorite commander, seek safety in headlong flight."[126] Jeb Stuart himself rallied elements of the 1st Virginia Cavalry as it retreated. With the Confederate cavalry chief cheering them on, the 1st Virginia briefly rallied and made a countercharge that brought the Federal pursuit to a halt.[127]

The two sides kept up skirmish and small arms fire until darkness fell. "Stuart had no fresh troops with which to renew the fight; he therefore maintained his position until night, when he withdrew to the York turnpike, leaving the 1st Virginia on picket on the field," stated Maj. Henry B. McClellan, Stuart's adjutant general.[128]

"As darkness came that night," a Federal recalled, "all was still in our front, except an occasional shot or shell, as the gunners still tried to get the range in the deepening gloom, which was settling down on the bloody field, where the killed and wounded laid in heaps, literally piled in swaths." Custer rejoined Kilpatrick on the Federal left flank, leaving Gregg's two brigades to maintain their lonely vigil at the critical crossroads of the Hanover and Low Dutch roads.[129]

The fight for East Cavalry Field ended with David Gregg's men still stubbornly in place.

*   *   *

All told, the battle for East Cavalry Field had lasted about three hours. The bulk of that time was spent in dismounted skirmishing, with the mounted phase ending quickly. The grand Confederate charge and the resulting melee lasted only 15 or 20 minutes. "Mounted fights never lasted long, but there were more men killed and wounded in this fight than I ever saw on any field where the fighting was done mounted," recalled Sgt. Jerry

---

126 Wittenberg, *At Custer's Side*, 132.

127 "Statement of Sgt. Elliott G. Fishburne," *The Bachelder Papers*, 2:1,286.

128 McClellan, *The Life and Campaigns of Maj. Gen. J.E.B. Stuart*, 341.

129 Husby and Wittenberg, *Under Custer's Command*, 37; Brooke-Rawle, *Third Pennsylvania Cavalry*, 280.

Haden of the 1st Virginia Cavalry.[130] "The field is ours; the charge is ours," observed a victorious Wolverine, "and we are Michigan's. Not one inch do we fall back, but rally, reform, as steadily as if on parade. Comrades shake comrades' hands. Tears flow as we gather our dead. The wounded are cared for amid the thunder of battle, which is making great rents in the sky."[131] The 1st Michigan suffered heavy casualties in making its gallant charge. "Without doubt several of the boys of the First were killed and more wounded by our own battery," observed Lieutenant Harris, "but it was absolutely necessary to break that charge at any cost, for if it succeeded there were no Union troops between the rebels and our ammunition trains."[132] Another Wolverine of the 7th Michigan Cavalry echoed a similar note, bragging, "Cavalry never did such fighting before in America."[133]

David Gregg's worst fears had been borne out, but his men had fairly met the heavy task they faced that morning. They met the unequal odds head-on, and had won the day's brutal and critical contest.

130 Haden, *J.E.B. Stuart's Cavalry*, 25.

131 Bigelow, "The Michigan Cavalry Brigade at Gettysburg."

132 Harris, *The Michigan Brigade of Cavalry*, 16.

133 Andrew Newton Buck to his brother and sister, July 9, 1863, copy in files at GNMP.

Conclusion

The Union Cavalry's Finest Hour

The fighting for Brinkerhoff's Ridge on July 2 and East Cavalry Field on the following day bore the indelible thumb print of David Gregg, whose sound decisions and good tactics guided the Union cavalry to victory.

General Gregg greatly contributed to the Union victory along the right flank of the Army of the Potomac by keeping the veterans of the Stonewall Brigade out of the crucial fight for Culp's Hill on the late afternoon and evening of the battle's second day. During the successful fight for Brinkerhoff's Ridge, Gregg recognized the vulnerability of the Union right and the potential of a Confederate attack from the ground east of Cress Ridge. He also recognized the ridge's strategic significance and made excellent dispositions to defend the critical crossroads of the Hanover and Low Dutch roads. Gregg followed this up by making excellent use of terrain and expertly shifting his meager resources to meet serious enemy threats. Gregg conducted a stout fight on July 3 that defeated the best Southern troopers the Army of Northern Virginia's cavalry had to offer. His defensive fight that day on East Cavalry Field accomplished his goal of driving the Confederate cavalry back and protecting the army's flank and rear. "If, then, Gregg succeeded in resisting the attack made upon him by Stuart, it is evident that the victory belongs to and was properly claimed by him," asserted an officer of the 8th Pennsylvania Cavalry of Huey's brigade of

Gregg's division. His men recognized the value of their contribution on those hard-fought fields and were justifiably proud of it.[1]

The two sides suffered heavy casualties during the East Cavalry Field combat. Between McIntosh's brigade and Custer's Wolverines, the Yankee horse soldiers reported 254 casualties, with 219 of them in Custer's Michigan Brigade, the bulk of these in the 1st and 7th Michigan regiments.[2] The 1st Michigan alone sustained the loss of six officers and 80 enlisted men in just ten minutes of action that day—a testament to the ferocity of the fighting.[3]

Stuart reported 16 killed, 93 wounded, and 55 missing for losses totaling 164. This figure does not include Witcher's men. The next morning, Witcher could only muster 96 of out of 332, indicating losses of 236 in the 34th Battalion alone.[4] An officer of the 14th Virginia estimated that the contingents of the 14th and 16th Virginia suffered 25 percent losses, meaning that Witcher's command may have taken more than 300 casualties in their ferocious firefight with Alger's 5th Michigan. In short, Gregg inflicted more than 450 casualties on Stuart's vaunted cavalry.[5]

The battlefield was a dreadful place once the fight ended. Dead and wounded men and horses mingled promiscuously all over the ground. When he returned homes after the fighting, John Rummel saw one sight in particular that stayed with him the rest of his days. The bodies of a private of the 3rd Pennsylvania and a Confederate lay intertwined. The pair had fought each other on horseback and had cut each other down with their sabers. They

---

1   J. Edward Carpenter, "Gregg's Cavalry at Gettysburg," *Annals of the War Written by Leading Participants North & South* (Philadelphia Weekly Times Pub. Co., 1879), 530.

2   *OR* 27, pt. 1, 957.

3   Robertson, *Michigan in the War*, 576.

4   Witcher, "Chambersburg Raid." It bothered Witcher a great deal that his command did not receive credit for its performance that day when Stuart penned his report of the campaign. "You naturally ask why these facts were not published before," he wrote. "The answer is soon given. After returning to Virginia, the Thirty-fourth was detached and sent to southwest Virginia, and I was never called upon to make an official report of the operations of the troops under my command during or after the campaign." Ibid.

5   *OR* 27, pt. 2, 714-715; Witcher to Bachelder, various letters, *The Bachelder Papers*, 2:1,229, 1,236, 1,298, and 3:1,480; Bouldin to Bachelder, various letters, *The Bachelder Papers*, 3:1,439-1,445 and 3:1,447. Capt. Edward E. Bouldin of the 14th Virginia Cavalry noted that "a very large per cent of the men and officers engaged were killed or wounded." Bouldin, "Charlotte Cavalry."

lay with their feet together, their heads in opposite directions, but their blood-stained sabres still clutched tightly in death. In another place, Rummel found a Virginian and yet another trooper of the 3rd Pennsylvania. They, too, had fought mounted with their sabres until they finally grabbed onto one another and their horses ran from under them. Their heads and shoulders were severely slashed, and their fingers, "though stiff in death, were so firmly embedded in each other's flesh that they could not be removed without the aid of force." In addition, Rummel found thirty dead horses on his property alone.[6]

Major William G. Connor was killed in action. His last words, as reported by a Union prisoner of war, were that he was a major of the Jeff Davis Legion. "It was a sad day for the Legion, as they all mourn the loss of Major Connor," reported Pvt. Joseph Dunbar Shields, Jr. "In him we lost a fine officer and a good man. We miss him very much."[7] Lieutenant Colonel J. Fred Waring, the commander of the Little Jeff, as the Jeff Davis Legion was known, was also wounded in the melee.

Sergeant William Brownlee of Company A of the Jeff Davis Legion was also killed in the melee. "In losing Brownlee we lost a noble man, he was loved and respected by all who knew him," lamented Shields. "Everybody placed the greatest confidence in him, he made a good soldier and officer. We all felt his death very much." Brownlee's company commander, Capt. Thomas Jefferson Adams, and two enlisted men drew the sad task of burying the sergeant on the field.[8]

Corporal Horace Barse of Company E, 5th Michigan Cavalry, 18 years old and from Detroit, received a mortal abdominal wound during the fighting for the Rummel farm. His brother, 22-year-old Lt. George R. Barse, found his dreadfully wounded brother lying on the field once the fighting petered out. George took Horace to a nearby home that had been impressed into service as a field hospital, where the attending surgeon declared the wound mortal. George told his brother that he was going to die, and was surprised when his brother showed no emotion. George then informed him

---

6 Brooke-Rawle, *Third Pennsylvania Cavalry*, 313-314.

7 Joseph Dunbar Shields, Jr. to My Kate, July 20, 1863, included in Elizabeth Dunbar Murray, *My Mother Used to Say: A Natchez Belle of the Sixties* (Boston: Christopher Publishing House, 1959), 176.

8 Ibid.

that he had to leave with his regiment, and asked whether Horace had any final message for their parents. Horace met his gaze and replied, "Yes, Tell Father and Mother that I died doing my duty in a noble cause, and that I am contented."

Knowing that Horace had a sweetheart and surprised that he had not sent a message along for her, George asked, "Do you wish to send anything to anyone else?"

"Yes," replied Horace, "tell Emily the same." Pulled away by his duty, George left Horace, whom he never saw again.[9]

Lieutenant William Brooke-Rawle of the 3rd Pennsylvania Cavalry summed up the feelings of the Yankee troopers:

> We cavalrymen have always held that we saved the day at the most critical moment of the Battle of Gettysburg—the greatest battle and turning point of the War of the Rebellion. Had Stuart succeeded in his well-laid plan, and, with his large force of cavalry, struck the Army of the Potomac in the rear of its line of battle, simultaneously with Pickett's magnificent and furious assault on its front, when our infantry had all it could do to hold on to the line of Cemetery Ridge, and but little more was needed to make the assault a success, the merest tyro in the art of war can readily tell what the result would have been. Fortunately for us; fortunately for the Army of the Potomac; fortunately for our Country and the cause of human liberty, he failed. Thank God that he did fail, and that, with His Divine Assistance, the good fight fought here brought victory to our arms![10]

"Charging in close column, the troopers using the saber only, the host of rebel myrimonds were immediately swept from the field," raved Colonel Town in his after-action report. "Never before in the history of this war has one regiment of National cavalry met an entire brigade of Confederate

9 E. A. Paul, "Operations of Our Cavalry: The Michigan Cavalry Brigade," *New York Times*, August 6, 1863. Once the Army of Northern Virginia had re-crossed the Potomac River into Virginia, Lieutenant Barse sought and received permission to return to Gettysburg to retrieve his fallen brother's body so that it could be taken home to Detroit for burial. The lowest price he could find for someone to transport the corpse thirty miles to the train station was the large sum of $60.00, which Barse paid. By contrast, his lieutenant's pay was probably in the range of $30.00 per month.

10 Brooke-Rawle, *Third Pennsylvania Cavalry*, 290-291.

cavalry . . . in open field—in a charge and defeated them. By the blessing of God, they were not only defeated, but they were driven from the field in great confusion, and this regiment held the ground until ordered to a new position." Colonel Town praised his officers and men for their gallant performance that day, noting that they had been outnumbered by odds of five to one. He wrote, "That each did his duty is verified by the fact that the loss of the regiment in ten minutes was six officers and eighty men."[11] The veterans of the 1st Michigan were rightly proud of their performance. "This is the most furious dragoon fight I ever saw or engaged in," proclaimed Pvt. Dexter Macomber.[12]

Colonel Russell A. Alger of the 5th Michigan Cavalry had a clear view of the charge. "I cannot pass the notice of this charge of the 1st Cavalry without adding a word to its already recorded well-earned praise," he wrote. "I do not believe it had its equal during the war, if ever. The squadrons, with almost faultless alignment, were hurled upon the largely superior numbers of the enemy, and as each squadron came up it was broken and forced out on either flank of the succeeding one, which filled its place, until over one-half of the regiment was broken up." He noted that the already exhausted Confederates, worn out from their eight-day ordeal on the way to Gettysburg, "could not stand such terrible and rapid blows, and were forced to leave the field in haste and confusion, while the broken squadron of the gallant 1st formed as best they could in the rear of their regiment and joined in the pursuit."[13]

The men of the 1st Michigan had sealed their place in history with their determined charge. "I cannot find language to express my high appreciation of the gallantry and daring displayed by the officers and men of the First Michigan cavalry," wrote Custer. "They advanced to the charge of a vastly superior force with as much order and precision as if going upon parade; and I challenge the annals of warfare to produce a more brilliant or successful charge of cavalry than the one just recounted."[14] A Federal artillerist

11 Wittenberg, *At Custer's Side*, 116.

12 Dexter Macomber diary, copy in files, Gettysburg National Military Park, entry for July 3, 1863.

13 Robertson, *Michigan in the War*, 578-579.

14 Wittenberg, *At Custer's Side*, 132.

overheard a captured Rebel officer say, "if Stuart knew how strong you were here he would soon have you routed out of this." Indeed, continued the Federal's account, "and very fortunate it was that he did not know how strong we were, or we might have got worsted in the affair."[15]

Captain James H. Kidd, who spent most of his postwar life chronicling the exploits of the Michigan Cavalry Brigade, gave all of the credit for the victory to David Gregg. Kidd noted that there was no mistake about the Federal cavalry's presence in the right place at the right time that day. "It was Gregg's prescience," wrote Kidd, who continued:

> He saw the risk of attempting to guard the right flank with only the two decimated brigades of his own division. If Custer's presence on the field was, as often has been said, 'providential,' it is General D. M. Gregg to whom, under Providence, the credit for bringing him there was due. . . . We can see that the engagement which he fought on the right at Gettysburg, on July 3, 1863, was from first to last, a well planned battle, in which the different commands were maneuvered with the same sagacity displayed by a skillful chess player in moving the pawns upon a chessboard; in which ever detail was the fruit of the brain of one man, who from the time he turned Custer to the northward, until he sent the First Michigan thundering against the brigades of Hampton and Fitzhugh Lee, made not a single false move; who was distinguished not less for his intuitive foresight than for his quick perceptions at critical moments. That man was General David McMurtrie Gregg.[16]

While Kidd's assessment was correct, David Gregg was far too modest to claim the credit for himself. "Stuart with 4 Brigades of Cavalry, intended to effect a surprise upon the rear of our Army, & to do this proposed to occupy the two Brigades of the 2nd Division & Custer's Michigan Brigade with sharpshooters, & quietly slip the bulk of his command between our position & the main army. The intended surprise was admirably planned but execution was difficult, if not impossible for two reasons," wrote Gregg in 1907. "In the first place the Union Cavalry in his front, fresh from recent

15 Townsend diary, 49.

16 Kidd, *Personal Recollections*, 137-138.

victories, did not propose to be entertained by a line of sharpshooters, & as will be discovered later, it forced the fighting & brought about that serious entanglement of which Gen. Stuart speaks, & then too, his design was fully penetrated, & hence it was that during the severe fighting that followed, Col. Irvin Gregg's 2nd Brigade was held in reserve & required to picket with a strong line from our position to the right of our main army."[17]

General Gregg remained in command of his Second Cavalry Division until February 1865, when he resigned his commission under questionable and uncertain circumstances. At times, the soft-spoken horse soldier commanded the entire Cavalry Corps and did so competently. In 1864, when Maj. Gen. Philip H. Sheridan assumed command of the Army of Potomac's Cavalry Corps, he leaned heavily on Gregg, who was his most experienced division commander. Although we do not know the reasons why Gregg resigned his commission, he was a great loss to the Army of the Potomac and to the Regular Army. He never served again.[18]

Colonel John B. McIntosh became one of the most respected horse soldiers in either army. He was badly injured during the fall of 1863, but returned and played a prominent role in the spring and summer campaigns of 1864. After returning to duty, he received such a severe wound at Third Winchester in September of 1864 that his leg was amputated. In spite of his wound, McIntosh received a promotion to brigadier general of volunteers and gained the respect of all who served under him. He was a fine soldier with an excellent career in the mounted service.

Despite being overshadowed by the grand infantry fighting, the critical role played by the Federal cavalry operating on the Army of the Potomac's right flank during the second and third days of Gettysburg were noted by early historians. The Comte de Paris, who observed the battle while serving

17 Gregg, "Second Cavalry Division," 13-14.

18 Gregg was too much of a gentleman to go into detail, and there is no written record of his reasons other than his letter of resignation, in which he stated that he was needed at home as a result of pressing family business. Sheridan, who had almost no experience commanding cavalry, was promoted over Gregg, and Gregg undoubtedly resented that. Thereafter, Gregg watched while Sheridan wrecked the military careers of his West Point classmates and friends, Brig. Gens. William Woods Averell and Alfred T. A. Torbert over niggling matters; Gregg undoubtedly feared that he would be next. By February 1865, it was obvious that the end of the war was approaching, and Gregg probably realized that sooner or later, he would end up under Sheridan's command once more. It seems likely that he resigned in order to avoid serving under Sheridan's command again.

as a volunteer aide to Maj. Gen. George Meade, observed that the Federal cavalry had "accomplished their object and frustrated the plan of their adversaries. By their first attack, and subsequently by their vigorous resistance, they have interrupted Stuart's flank movement."[19]

The Federal cavalry gained confidence every day under solid leadership. "Brigadier Generals Merritt and Custer, brigade commanders, have increased the confidence entertained in their ability and gallantry to lead troops on the field of battle," Cavalry Corps commander Pleasonton opined.[20] A Pennsylvanian of Gregg's division agreed: "The cavalry under Pleasonton and Kilpatrick have been doing noble service ever since crossing the Potomac."[21]

General Custer also received plaudits for his role that day. "Custer was in his glory that day, if ever," recalled a Pennsylvania horse soldier, "and the Michigan Brigade proved itself to be the equal of any brigade in the service."[22] Custer had earned the respect of the horse soldiers of both sides with his reckless daring-do in leading charges. "Our boy-general never says 'Go in, men!'" recounted a Wolverine, "He says, with that whoop and yell of his, 'Come on, boys!' and in we go, you bet."[23] Before long, he would earn their love as well as their respect.

Custer, however, was still quite inexperienced at Gettysburg. Upon careful review of the historical record, it is clear that David Gregg did not yet fully trust the young brigadier. When Gregg ordered the charges of the 1st and 7th Michigan Cavalry during the climactic phases of the battle, he issued the orders to charge directly to the regimental commanders, bypassing Custer's authority over his own brigade. Although Custer bravely joined the charges of the Wolverines on East Cavalry Field, he actually had little to do with their success. That changed as he gained experience and respect. Custer

19 Louis Phillipe Albert d'Orleans, *Comte de Paris, History of the Civil War in America*, 3 vols. (Philadelphia: Porter & Coates, 1883), 3:679.

20 *OR* 27, pt. 1, 918.

21 Thomas Lucas to his wife, July 4, 1863, Thomas Lucas Letter, Dona Sauerburger Collection, Gambrills, MD.

22 John D. Follmer to John B. Bachelder, October 28, 1884, *The Bachelder Papers*, 2:1,075.

23 Elizabeth Bacon Custer, *Tenting on the Plains, or General Custer in Kansas and Texas* (Norman: University of Oklahoma Press, 1971), 9-10.

led the Wolverines into battle until October 1864, when he was promoted to command of a division of cavalry.

East Cavalry Field forever sealed the reputation of the Michigan Cavalry Brigade. Referring to the Michigan Brigade, correspondent Edward A. Paul of the *New York Times* correctly observed, "These regiments, taken as a whole, will compare favorably with any cavalry regiments. The officers and men for the most part are those who, by entering the service, made large sacrifices, and who were prompted to the step by as patriotic motives as ever inspired the breast of a true lover of his country. Soldiering with them is not a pastime, a spree, or a holiday, but a duty; and men thus animated, whatever they attempt to do is well done."[24] And so it was. Indeed, the Wolverines did their duty superbly that day.

Gregg and Custer also owed a large debt of gratitude to the superb work done by Pennington and Randol that day. Their batteries plainly demonstrated the superiority of the Federal horse artillery. "It is to be doubted if in the whole war there was an example of clear headed direction, skillful handling and gallant bearing of officers and men more brilliant than that of Company M in this action," noted a commentator on the performance of Pennington's battery.[25] "Our success in driving the enemy from the field is due, in a great measure to the highly efficient manner in which [Battery M, 2nd U.S. Artillery] was handled by Lieutenant A. C. M. Pennington, assisted by Lieutenants Clark, Woodruff, and Hamilton," correctly observed Custer.[26]

Captain John C. Tidball, a West Point-trained career artillerist who commanded a brigade of horse artillery assigned to serve with the Army of the Potomac's Cavalry Corps, summarized the action after the war. "An obstinate fight between the opposing cavalries here took place, not of such magnitude perhaps as some other cavalry battles," explained Tidball, "but certainly of great moment to the welfare of the Union cause. In it the horse batteries of Randol and Pennington took an unusually important part; in fact

24 Quoted in Robertson, *Michigan in the War*, 587.

25 Samuel A. Ashe, Stephen B. Weeks, and Charles L. Van Noppen, eds., *Biographical History of North Carolina from Colonial Times to the Present*, 8 vols. (Greensboro, NC: Charles L. Van Noppen, 1907), 6:507.

26 Robertson, *Michigan in the War*, 584.

so much so that without them Stuart would probably have gained his object."[27]

Some of the Wolverines, who had not seen much combat prior to the beginning of the Gettysburg campaign, commented, "such fighting I never saw before," and "cavalry never did such fighting before in America."[28] "I was very anxious to have one big fight before the war should end & that fight I got at Gettysburg. I never want to see another one," observed a trooper of the 7th Michigan, who saw his first major engagement on East Cavalry Field.[29] The Michigan men became perhaps the finest single brigade of cavalry in the Union service, and saw combat on many more fields over the duration of the war.

In retrospect, it seems obvious that Stuart intended to ambush the Federal horsemen. Would Stuart, with his men and horses as tired as they were, seriously have considered placing himself between Gregg's men and the bulk of the Army of the Potomac's infantry, and then turn his back on Gregg? While doing so would have been audacious, it also would have been a foolish invitation to annihilation. If his men and horses had been fresh, his doing so might have been conceivable, though unlikely. Even with well-rested men and horses, it would have been like riding into a bottle, with Gregg's men playing the role of the cork. Instead, an ambush aimed at crushing Gregg's men makes far more sense under the circumstances. Stuart had the Northern horsemen outnumbered and isolated from the main body of the Army of the Potomac.

If he had succeeded in crushing Gregg, he could then operate with impunity in the Union rear. Further, if the Pickett-Pettigrew-Trimble charge succeeded, the unopposed presence of Confederate cavalry would be all the more devastating. Therefore, although Stuart never really explained his reasons for being where he was, analysis and logic points to the fact that he intended to ambush Gregg's Federals, and that the attempted ambush failed.

Major William A. Morgan, who commanded a battalion of the 1st Virginia Cavalry of Fitz Lee's brigade, criticized the timeliness of Stuart's

27 John C. Tidball, "Artillery Service in the War of the Rebellion," Part V, *Journal of the Military Service Institution of the United States*, 13 (July 1892), 695.

28 Wert, *Gettysburg: Day Three*, 271.

29 William H. O'Brien to his brother, October 21, 1863, O'Brien Family Papers, Bentley Historical Library, University of Michigan, Ann Arbor.

actions on July 3. He pointed out that neither Stuart nor the infantry began their attacks before noon. "This half-day's inactivity seemed to be participated in by the entire army, as far as I could learn—a most fatal mistake that cost the fearful and immense loss we sustained in the afternoon, the disastrous termination of the Pennsylvania Campaign, and the return of a dispirited army to Virginia," he complained. "Had the cavalry been in their saddle at daylight, striking for the rear of the enemy's position; had the immortal Pickett led his brave division up that fatal slope early in the morning, and before the enemy had had time to concentrate and fortify their strong position, the result might have been different."[30]

Despite his failure to ambush David Gregg on East Cavalry Field, Jeb Stuart still successfully protected the Confederate left flank and prevented it from being turned. His presence on that flank likely prevented Gregg's two brigades from moving into the Confederate rear and making mischief of their own there. Stuart performed magnificently during the retreat from Gettysburg. His scouting and screening of the Confederate march back to Virginia was flawless.[31] He remained at the head of his troopers until the Battle of Yellow Tavern on May 11, 1864, when a Wolverine mortally wounded him in combat. However, by that time the tide had already turned. Never again would his horse soldiers run roughshod over the Army of the Potomac's Cavalry Corps. From the end of the Gettysburg campaign until the conclusion of the Civil War, the two forces often met as equals.

Stuart's command was in wretched condition on July 3. "My company has dwindled down to 10 or 15 the horses of the rest having completely broken down," reported a captain of 3rd Virginia Cavalry on July 5. "Have unsaddled our horses only for two nights of the fortnight."[32] A member of the Jeff Davis Legion noted a few days later, "We have not had over 150 or two hundred mounted and fit for duty and since then we have lost killed,

---

30 Morgan, "Desperate Charges."

31 For a detailed discussion of the fighting, and of Stuart's magnificent work during the retreat from Gettysburg, see Eric J. Wittenberg, J. David Petruzzi, and Michael F. Nugent, *One Continuous Fight: The Retreat from Gettysburg and the Pursuit of Lee's Army of Northern Virginia, July 4-14, 1863* (New York, NY: Savas-Beatie, 2008).

32 Jeff Toalson, ed., *Send Me a Pair of Old Boots & Kiss My Little Girls: The Civil War Letters of Richard and Mary Watkins, 1861-1865* (New York: iUniverse, 2009), 203.

wounded, missing or prisoners, about seventy or eighty."[33] When he penned his report of the campaign, Stuart admitted that, "some regiments were reduced to 100 men; yet when my command arrived at Gettysburg, from the accessions which it received from the weak horses left to follow the command, it took its place in line of battle with a stoutness of heart and firmness of tread impressing one with the confidence of victory which was astounding, considering the hardness of the march lately endured."[34] Obviously, the heavy fighting on East Cavalry Field only further wore down men and animals, but given the ordeal that they had just been through, these men fought hard at Gettysburg and even harder during the retreat to Virginia after the end of the battle in Pennsylvania—a testament to their fortitude and dependability.

Wade Hampton recovered from his Gettysburg wounds and resumed his duties at the head of his command. Withal, Hampton kept his sense of humor. Thirteen days after receiving his Gettysburg wounds, he penned a letter to his sister. "My head is well externally," he wrote, "but seems tender inside; perhaps it is only weak. The penitentiary style in which my hair is cut, half the head being shaven, is striking, if not beautiful," he wrote, tongue planted firmly in cheek. "It suits all kinds of weather, as one side of my head, is sure to be just right, either for cool, or for hot weather. But the flies play the mischief, as they wander over the bald side. When I get home, I will shave my whole head, to be uniform at least. Don't you feel mortified that any Yankee should be able, on horseback, to split my head open? It shows how old I am growing, and how worthless."[35] Fortunately for the Southern mounted arm, Hampton was wrong about his prowess and worth to the Confederacy. When he returned to duty in September 1863, Hampton was promoted to major general and given a division when Stuart's cavalry was reorganized into a corps of three divisions. He took permanent command of the Army of Northern Virginia's Cavalry Corps in August 1864 after Stuart

---

33 Murray, *My Mother Used to Say*, 177.

34 *OR* vol. 27, pt. 2, 709. Stuart reported that his command suffered an aggregate loss of about 2,200 killed, wounded, and missing from Brandy Station to the end of the Gettysburg Campaign.

35 Charles E. Cauthen, ed., *Family Letters of the Three Wade Hamptons 1782-1901* (Columbia: University of South Carolina Press, 1953), 94.

fell earlier that spring. By the end of the war Hampton was a lieutenant general and had bested his Union rivals on nearly every battlefield.

Fitz Lee was also promoted to major general in the fall of 1863, and he commanded a division until the winter of 1865, when he became the Army of Northern Virginia's final Cavalry Corps commander. Lee received a severe leg wound at Third Winchester on September 19, 1864, and did not return to duty until after Hampton and his command were sent to South Carolina to resist the advance of Maj. Gen. William T. Sherman's army in February of 1865. Fitz Lee personally led the final charge of the Army of Northern Virginia's Cavalry Corps at Farmville, Virginia, on April 9, 1865—the same day his uncle Robert E. Lee surrendered the Army of Northern Virginia. After the war, Fitz Lee served as governor of Virginia and became one of several former Confederate commanders to return to duty in the U.S. Army for the Spanish-American War. He was commissioned a major general of volunteers and served as military governor of Havana and Pinar del Rio. Lee died April 28, 1905.

John Chambliss retained command of Rooney Lee's brigade throughout the retreat from Gettysburg and through the Bristoe Station and Mine Run campaigns during the fall and early winter of 1863, while Lee remained a prisoner of war. Chambliss received a brigadier general's wreath, but was killed in action in August of 1864. "The loss sustained by the cavalry in the fall of General Chambliss will be felt throughout the army, in which, by his courage, energy and skill, he had won for himself an honorable name," lamented Robert E. Lee.[36]

The battles for Brinkerhoff's Ridge and East Cavalry Field were small actions compared to the main battle that raged at Gettysburg. By almost any measure—number of men engaged, casualties, or rounds of ammunition expended—these two fights, taken alone, would not have impacted the outcome of the battle as a whole. Within their limitations, however, both were critical to the battle's progression. By making a successful attack against Brinkerhoff's Ridge, David Gregg prevented the Stonewall Brigade

36 Bergeron, Arthur W. "John Randolph Chambliss, Jr." included in William C. Davis and Julie Hoffman, eds.,*The Confederate General*, 6 vols. (Harrisburg, PA: National Historical Society, 1991), 1:173.Chambliss and David Gregg were good friends prior to the outbreak of the Civil War, and Chambliss was killed fighting against Gregg's troopers. His West Point class ring was recovered and delivered to Gregg, who made arrangements for it to be returned to his old friend's family.

from participating in the failed Confederate attacks on Culp's Hill, where the additional men might have tipped the balance in the Army of Northern Virginia's favor.

The actions on Brinkerhoff's Ridge and East Cavalry Field are often overlooked in historical treatments of the battle of Gettysburg and most battlefield tours today ignore them unless coverage is specifically requested. Hopefully, readers now have a much clearer understanding of the significance of these actions, and a deeper comprehension of the tactics employed and of the impact those tactics had on the outcome of the fighting. The fights for Brinkerhoff's Ridge and East Cavalry Field marked a major step in the evolution of the Army of the Potomac's Cavalry Corps into the finest mounted force ever to grace the North American continent.

Brinkerhoff's Ridge, Gettysburg, July 2, 1863

ARMY OF THE POTOMAC

Cavalry Corps
Maj. Gen. Alfred Pleasonton

Second Cavalry Division
Brig. Gen. David McMurtrie Gregg

First Brigade[1]
Col. John B. McIntosh

Purnell (Maryland) Legion, Company A
Capt. Robert E. Duvall

1st New Jersey Cavalry (9 companies)
Maj. Myron H. Beaumont

3rd Pennsylvania Cavalry
Lt. Col. Edward S. Jones

---

1 The 1st Massachusetts Cavalry was normally part of McIntosh's brigade. However, as a result of severe losses taken at the battle of Aldie on June 17, 1863, it was detached and was serving as headquarters escort for the VI Army Corps. Likewise, the 1st Pennsylvania Cavalry was detached and serving with the Second Army Corps on July 2, 1863.

Third Brigade[2]
Col. J. Irvin Gregg

10th New York Cavalry
Maj. M. Henry Avery

Artillery

3rd Pennsylvania Heavy Artillery, Battery H
(One Section: two 3-inch Ordnance Rifles)
Capt. William D. Rank

Total strength: 988 officers and men

ARMY OF NORTHERN VIRGINIA

Richard Ewell's Second Corps

Edward Johnson's Division

Stonewall Brigade
Brig. Gen. James Walker

2nd Virginia
Col. John Quincy Adams Nadenbousch

Total strength: 333 officers and men

---

2   The 4th Pennsylvania Cavalry of J. Irvin Gregg's brigade had been detached and sent to the center of the Union line on the afternoon of July 2 and did not participate in the fighting for Brinkerhoff's Ridge.

East Cavalry Field, Gettysburg, July 3, 1863

ARMY OF THE POTOMAC

Cavalry Corps
Maj. Gen. Alfred Pleasonton

Second Division
Brig. Gen. David McMurtrie Gregg

First Brigade[1]
Col. John B. McIntosh

1st Maryland Cavalry (11 companies)
Lt. Col. James M. Deems

Purnell (Maryland) Legion, Company A
Capt. Robert E. Duvall

1st New Jersey Cavalry (9 companies)
Maj. Myron H. Beaumont

3rd Pennsylvania Cavalry
Lt. Col. Edward S. Jones

---

1 The 1st Massachusetts Cavalry was part of McIntosh's brigade. Because of severe losses at Aldie on June 17, 1863, it was detached and was serving as headquarters escort for the VI Corps. The 1st Pennsylvania Cavalry was also detached and serving with Second Corps.

Third Brigade
Col. J. Irvin Gregg

1st Maine Cavalry
Lt. Col. Charles H. Smith
10th New York Cavalry
Maj. M. Henry Avery
16th Pennsylvania Cavalry
Lt. Col. John K. Robison

Third Division
Brig. Gen. Judson Kilpatrick

Second Brigade
Brig. Gen. George Armstrong Custer

1st Michigan Cavalry
Col. Charles H. Town

5th Michigan Cavalry (Col. Russell A. Alger)
6th Michigan Cavalry (Col. George Gray)
7th Michigan Cavalry (Col. William D'Alton Mann)

Horse Artillery

1st U.S. Horse Artillery, Batteries E and G
(four 12-pounder Napoleons) Capt. Alanson M. Randol

2nd U.S. Horse Artillery, Battery M
(six 3-inch Ordnance Rifles) Lt. Alexander Cummings McWhorter Pennington Jr.

Total strength: 3,936 officers and men

Total losses: 281 (14.1%)

ARMY OF NORTHERN VIRGINIA

Cavalry Division

Maj. Gen. James Ewell Brown Stuart

Hampton's Brigade
Brig. Gen. Wade Hampton (w)
Col. Laurence S. Baker

1st North Carolina Cavalry
(Col. Laurence S. Baker, Lt. Col. James B. Gordon)

1st South Carolina Cavalry (detachment)
Lt. Col. John D. Twiggs[2]

2nd South Carolina Cavalry
Maj. Thomas J. Lipscomb

Cobb's (Georgia) Legion
Col. Pierce Manning Butler Young

Jeff Davis (Mississippi) Legion
Lt. Col. Joseph Frederick Waring

Phillips' (Georgia) Legion
Lt. Col. William Wofford Rich

Fitzhugh Lee's Brigade
Brig. Gen. Fitzhugh Lee

1st Virginia Cavalry (Col. James H. Drake)
2nd Virginia Cavalry (Col. Thomas T. Munford)
3rd Virginia Cavalry (Col. Thomas H. Owen)
4th Virginia Cavalry (Col. Williams C. Wickham)
5th Virginia Cavalry (Col. Thomas L. Rosser)

---

2   Colonel John L. Black, wounded at Upperville, later stated that Maj. William Walker commanded the regiment at this time.

William Henry Fitzhugh Lee's Brigade
Col. John Randolph Chambliss, Jr.

2nd North Carolina Cavalry
Capt. William A. Graham, Jr. (w), Lt. Joseph Baker

9th Virginia Cavalry
Col. Richard L. T. Beale

10th Virginia Cavalry
(10 Companies) Col. James Lucius Davis

13th Virginia Cavalry
Capt. Benjamin F. Winfield

Jenkins' Brigade
(Detachment) Lt. Col. Vincent A. Witcher

14th Virginia Cavalry
Maj. Benjamin F. Eakle

16th Virginia Cavalry
Maj. James H. Nounnan

17th Virginia Cavalry
Col. William H. French

34th Battalion Virginia Cavalry
Lt. Col. Vincent A. Witcher

36th Battalion Virginia Cavalry
Capt. Cornelius T. Smith

Stuart Horse Artillery
Maj. Robert F. Beckham

Breathed's (Virginia) Battery, 1st Stuart Horse Artillery
(four 3-inch Ordnance Rifles), Capt. James Williams Breathed

McGregor's (Virginia) Battery, 2nd Stuart Horse Artillery
(one Blakely Rifle, one unknown), Capt. William M. McGregor

Jackson's (Virginia) Battery, Charlottesville Horse Artillery
(two 3-inch Ordnance Rifles, two 12-pounder Howitzers)
Capt. Thomas E. Jackson

Attached Artillery

Green's Battery, Louisiana Guard Artillery
(one section: two 10-pounder Parrotts) Capt. Charles A. Green[3]

Total strength: 6,702 reported, but only 4,807 actually present for duty
at East Cavalry Field

Total losses: 310 (6.4%)

---

3 Assigned to Ewell's Second Corps, but remained with the cavalry division after serving
with Wade Hampton's brigade at Hunterstown on July 2, 1863.

What was Jeb Stuart's Mission on July 3, 1863?

In 2005, Tom Carhart, a West Point-trained decorated combat veteran of the Vietnam War with a law degree and a doctorate in history, published a book entitled *Lost Triumph: Lee's Real Plan at Gettysburg and Why It Failed*[1] The book was met with acclaim by historians who, with the notable exception of Carhart's mentor Prof. James M. McPherson, are not generally known as authorities on the Civil War.

Many of these historians lauded Carhart's allegedly novel theories as follows:

(1) Jeb Stuart's actions on East Cavalry Field were intended to be specifically coordinated with the Pickett-Pettigrew-Trimble charge ("Pickett's Charge") against the Union center on the main battlefield;

(2) That the four shots fired by Stuart's artillery at the start of the engagement were intended as an announcement to Gen. Robert E. Lee that Stuart's command was in place and ready to attack; and

(3) Only George Armstrong Custer's heroics saved the Union.

---

1   Tom Carhart, *Lost Triumph: Lee's Real Plan at Gettysburg and Why It Failed* (New York: G. P. Putnam's Sons, 2005).

Gen. Robert E. Lee.
LC

I believe that not only is there nothing new about these theories, and that they are unsubstantiated by tangible evidence, but that available evidence *refutes* these theories.

What follows is the essence of Carhart's theories, in his own words[2]:

> I believe that, on the evening of July 2, Lee told Stuart that he wanted to convert the fight at Gettysburg into another Castiglione. In the late afternoon of July 2, Longstreet's attack against the Union left had been so powerful that it forced Meade to send troops there from other parts of his defensive position, in particular the XII Corps under Slocum from Culp's Hill. Six of the seven brigades in that corps were sent to prop up Longstreet (sic), leaving only the brigade under Greene in place. Johnson's attack against Culp's Hill started at about six o'clock that evening, but his three brigades made little headway against the well-entrenched men under Greene, who had been stiffened by some eight hundred men from Wadsworth's I Corps. Around nine o'clock, elements of the XII Corps, some 5,000 men, began to reappear on or near Culp's Hill and ended any hope of Johnson's three brigades taking the hill. But Lee would have told Stuart, on the night of July 2, that Longstreet and Ewell would continue their attacks on the morning of July 3.

> It was important that Ewell not attack Culp's Hill on the morning of July 3 before Longstreet launched his attack. This was because Lee hoped the large Union unit he had learned was moving down onto Cemetery Ridge from Culp's Hill (the XII Corps) to stave off Longstreet's attack on July 2 would stay there, or be brought back down there, thus weakening the defenses on the Union right wing. If that happened, Lee had already arranged for the three Confederate brigades in Johnson's Division at the bottom of Culp's Hill to be reinforced to seven brigades, or some 10,000 men. And with that force attacking

---

2   I quote Mr. Carhart in an effort to be scrupulously fair and for the purpose of objective scholarly criticism. I have endeavored to use only enough material from his book for readers to make their own unbiased judgment. I encourage readers to peruse his entire book should they desire to do so, and in the end reach their own conclusions on this historical debate.

from the front, even if some or all of the XII Corps had returned to Culp's Hill, he thought he could take Culp's Hill.

But to be sure the plan worked and the Union right wing would fall, Lee wanted Stuart to play the role of Fiorella at Castiglione and come up behind the Union right wing while it was being attacked from the front by Ewell. Lee told Stuart that timing was most important, that he had to let the attack mature until he got the signal from Lee. When that happened, he was to move down off Cress Ridge, follow Bonaughton [Low Dutch] Road to the Baltimore Pike, then turn right and race up to the rear of Culp's Hill.

Lee was leaving both his flanks naked, unprotected by cavalry. But Lee knew his adversary, and he was certain Meade was more worried about surviving a Confederate attack than formulating one of his own. He was confident, in other words, that his two open and unprotected flanks would not be tested by a major Yankee flank attack.

To carry off this flank maneuver, Lee would give Stuart command of his only other cavalry unit, Jenkins' brigade of some 1,000 mounted riflemen. These were mountain men from what would become West Virginia armed with the latest Enfield rifles and sword bayonets imported through the blockage from England. If needed, 6,000 of Stuart's horsemen could attack Culp's Hill from the rear, in which case it would quickly collapse. But there was also a possibility it would take much less to tip the scales.

As an initial blow, this force of Jenkins' mounted infantry would dismount behind Culp's Hill and attack the Union defenses on top of it from the rear. With a thousand howling and firing Rebels attacking from the rear while ten thousand attacked from the front, he was confident the Union line would collapse and that he could then roll up the Union right wing. But if more was needed, Stuart had another five thousand men to throw in, though just having them gallop by screaming while Jenkins' men mounted their attack might do the trick. That would be up to Stuart.

As the barbed end of the Union Fishhook began to collapse thereafter, he would have Stuart's other three brigades of cavalry, some 5,000 mounted men, just move down the Union line and attack the Union troops on Cemetery Hill and between Cemetery Hill and Culp's Hill from the rear while they were attacked from the front by Early's Division, then by Rodes' Division, and eventually by all three divisions of A. P. Hill's corps. And as they moved along the rear of the Union line, one of the first things they would have done would be to kill or drive away from their guns the artillery crews, an easy task for a mounted man who came up behind them armed with carbine, saber, and revolver, all the more so since artillerymen wore no side arms behind friendly lines.

Stuart could then bring the crews from his own guns with him and use them to handle some of these guns. It would take only three or four men for each gun, and they would lower their muzzles and fire canister into the rear of the waiting Union infantry manning the defenses all along the line. Lee and Stuart would also have discussed the psychological power of six thousand Confederate cavalry crashing through the Union rear, filling the air with gunfire, explosions, and the high-pitched Rebel Yell that shook Yankee souls, all this occurring in what the Union soldiers would have thought was their safe and protected rear area. Such a surprise for the Yankees should have a stunning, heart-stopping, paralyzing impact.

The effect of these thousands of shooting, screaming horsemen loose in the Yankee rear would be far greater than that brought on by the few Guides and four bugles Napoleon had gotten behind Austrian lines at the Battle of Arcola, a small force that panicked them into fleeing to the rear. But, the Union army in the hook of the Fishhook, attacked front and rear, would have nowhere to go, and mass surrender would be their only option. The result would be the elimination of the northern half of the Army of the Potomac.

Meanwhile, the three divisions of Longstreet's corps would have been attacking the Union's left wing, just as they had done the day before. But this would only be a pinning or holding attack, just to make sure the Union forces in front of them—hopefully including the bulk of the XII

Corps, drawn down from Culp's Hill the day before—didn't flood north to rescue the men in blue who would quickly be going under.

Meade's troops were all deployed on the Fishhook line, save only the VI Corps. This was a fresh unit, Meade's reserve, and he kept it behind Little Round Top. If all these attacks occurred at once, the VI Corps probably would be used to stave off Longstreet's Corps, which had been the greatest threat on July 2. Thereafter, as the Union troops at the northern end surrendered and their conquerors turned south, the other half of Meade's army would now suddenly be heavily outnumbered and would have, in their turn, either surrendered or scattered.[3]

First, there is nothing novel about a theory claiming that Stuart's mission was to be a strike down the Low Dutch Road to the Baltimore Pike in order to coordinate with the Pickett-Pettigrew-Trimble assault on the Union center. Participants in the battle, such as James H. Kidd and William Brooke-Rawle, both made similar claims in the years immediately following the battle. Brooke-Rawle, in fact, claimed that the cavalry saved the Union that day. Perhaps these men overstated their role in their effort to aggrandize the importance of the clash of cavalry on July 3, and Carhart bought into these overstatements.

In 1970, in the first modern monograph on the battle on East Cavalry Field, historian David Riggs wrote that "Stuart's plan of battle for July 3 was vital to the anticipated victory of the Army of Northern Virginia. When General George Pickett . . . led an infantry charge of 15,000 men on the Federal center at Cemetery Ridge, Stuart would simultaneously attack the Federal rear and, hopefully, turn the right flank."[4]

In 2002, another Vietnam veteran named Paul D. Walker published a small tome that purported to address the fighting on East Cavalry Field. This poorly-written short effort offers very few primary sources and only includes fifteen pages dedicated to the fight between Gregg and Stuart. "The scheme of operations for the battle," opines Walker, "was for Generals Pickett, Pettigrew, and Trimble, with their three divisions, to advance on the

3   Ibid., 158-161.

4   Riggs, *East of Gettysburg*, 31.

same line and seize the center of the Union line. . . . Jeb Stuart would be sent to Meade's rear to prepare to attack the Federal rear when Pickett, Pettigrew or Trimble achieved a breakthrough."[5]

Clearly, Carhart's theory concerning the role to be played by Stuart is not original—other than the mistaken idea that the Confederate cavalry would attack up Culp's Hill and that Stuart would then use his horse artillerists to man the Union artillery. That aspect of the theory is novel for the simple reason that it is wholly implausible.

Further, there is not a scintilla of reliable evidence to support the theory that Stuart's cavalry thrust was coordinated with the grand Southern attack against Cemetery Ridge. Jeb Stuart's own words, taken from his official report about his mission that day, are revealing:

> On the morning of July 3, pursuant to instructions from the commanding general (the ground along our line of battle being totally impracticable for cavalry operations), I moved forward to a position to the left of . . . Ewell's left, and in advance of it, where a commanding ridge [Cress Ridge] completely controlled a wide plain of cultivated fields stretching toward Hanover, on the left, and reaching to the base of the mountain spurs, among which the enemy held position . . . I . . . *hoped to effect a surprise upon the enemy's rear.* . . . During this day's operations, I held such a position as not only to render Ewell's left entirely secure, where the firing of my command, mistaken for that of the enemy, caused some apprehension, but commanded a view of the routes leading to the enemy's rear. Had the enemy's main body been dislodged, as was confidently hoped and expected, I was in precisely the right position to discover it and improve the opportunity. I watched keenly and anxiously the indications in his rear for that purpose, which in the attack which I intended (which was forestalled by our troops being exposed to view), his cavalry would have separated from the main body, and gave promise of solid results and advantages. (emphasis added)[6]

5 Paul D. Walker, *The Cavalry Battle that Saved the Union: Custer vs. Stuart at Gettysburg* (Gretna, LA: Pelican Publishing Co., 2002), 135-136.

6 *OR* 27, pt. 2, 697, 699.

It is instructive and revealing that nowhere in this report does Stuart say his orders were anything other than to cover Ewell's flank and watch for an opportunity to make mischief in the Union rear. The "orders" described by Carhart simply do not exist. Further, what Stuart describes— trying to harass a broken and defeated enemy—is precisely one of the primary roles assigned to cavalry on any active battlefield.

General Lee's own report also does not mention any such scheme to coordinate Stuart with the infantry assault. Lee's military secretary, Col. Charles Marshall, who wrote most of Lee's after-action reports, also penned the report for the army's operations in the Gettysburg campaign. Nowhere does Lee mention anything like the theory described by Carhart. After describing the plan for the attacks of July 2 that nearly succeeded, Marshall wrote (at Lee's instruction), "These partial successes determined me to continue the assault the next day. Pickett, with three of his brigades, joined Longstreet the following morning, and our batteries were moved forward to the positions gained by him the day before. The general plan of attack was unchanged, excepting that one division and two brigades of Hill's corps were ordered to support Longstreet."[7]

This means that the original plan for the day did not include the Pickett-Pettigrew-Trimble charge, but rather a continuation of the prior day's attacks, which nearly broke the Federal line. If those plans changed, there was no way for Stuart to know of those revised plans since there was no communication between Stuart and the main body of the Confederate army. There is no mention of Stuart's operations on July 3 anywhere in this report, other than to say that "the day after its [Stuart's cavalry] arrival at Gettysburg it engaged the enemy's cavalry with unabated spirit, and effectually protected our left."[8] The words "effectually protected our left" comports perfectly with Stuart's report.

---

7 Ibid., 308.

8 Ibid., 322. It is important to note that Marshall firmly believed Stuart should have been court-martialed for his perceived failure to obey Lee's orders during the days leading up to the battle of Gettysburg. Marshall, in fact, said that he believed that Stuart should have been shot. Given that, it's difficult to believe that the orders invented by Carhart existed. Marshall spent years trashing Stuart in public and in print, and most assuredly would have used such tempting ammunition to prove his point. However, Marshall never mentioned anything pertaining to Stuart's performance once on the field at Gettysburg. Marshall's numerous critiques of Stuart are described in great detail in Wittenberg and Petruzzi, *Plenty of Blame to Go Around*, 183-199.

Undeterred by the lack of any mention (let alone evidence) in the official Confederate reports, Carhart manufactured an argument to justify his theory:

> If this high-risk venture didn't work for some unexpected reason, then no one other than Lee and Stuart and Ewell and Johnson, and perhaps a few brigade commanders and staff officers, would have known about it. And since it would not benefit the South to announce a flank attack attempted by Lee at Gettysburg, a high-risk flank attack that had failed, it would never be heard of again.[9]

"I think there can be little question," Carhart writes later regarding the lack of reports by Stuart's command, "that they were suppressed by order of General Robert E. Lee. . . . Nothing good for the South could come out of Lee admitting to anyone that he had tried to run a Union wing with a cavalry-infantry combination, and then to cut the Union force in half and defeat it in detail, but that this effort had failed."[10]

Carhart's allegation, predicated on supposition upon supposition, is simply not credible. Stuart's supposed flank attack failed, so Lee and Stuart (and anyone else "in on the scheme," so to speak) secretly agreed to never mention it. No other example of a similar clandestine agreement between Lee and his subordinates during the entire war has ever surfaced. If Lee wanted to "suppress" the embarrassment of Stuart's failure, why did he not try to "cover up" the much more substantial and embarrassing Pickett-Pettigrew-Trimble Charge—or any other failed effort that took place under his command during the war?

Carhart continues his claims with this declaration: "And the worst part of all was that it had failed because Jeb Stuart and his Invincibles, the flower of southern horsemen, had been stopped by a Yankee cavalry unit less than half its size. No, that was bad news no matter how you looked at it. And if it were ever made public, it would only boost the morale of Union forces at the same time administering a major blow to that of Confederate forces. So Lee

---

9   Carhart, *Lost Triumph*, 162.

10   Ibid., 244-245.

just swallowed it and never mentioned it to anyone."[11] Documentary evidence isn't necessary when you can read Robert E. Lee's mind.

Carhart has a law degree and knows about burdens of proof. Declaring something as the truth without viable evidence to support that declaration does not meet any burden of proof. Attorneys are fond of saying something along these lines: "If the facts are on your side, pound the facts into the table; if the law is on your side, pound the law into the table; if neither are on your side, just pound the table." Carhart's arguments are the equivalent of wishful table pounding.

In the absence of any reliable evidence to the contrary, we have to take Lee's and Stuart's reports at their word. When reading the two reports together, it is clear that Stuart's orders and intentions were to operate on the Confederate left flank, to secure Ewell's flank, and to ambush and defeat Gregg. If he could defeat Gregg, then and only then would an opportunity present itself to make mischief in the Union rear (regardless of any failure or success by the Rebel infantry on the main battlefield). Stuart watched Gregg's Second Division from Brinkerhoff's Ridge the previous day. He knew the Union horsemen were there, and ambushing them became his objective. Anything else is speculation devoid of any historical evidence whatsoever to support it. Carhart's theory is an armchair general's fantasy, and nothing more.

For Carhart's theory to work, Stuart's large force would have had to move behind the Union rear undetected. On a hot summer day, thousands of horses kick up billowing clouds of dust that can be seen from miles away. Indeed, the Federal XI Corps spotted Stuart's movement and reported it to headquarters, intelligence that was timely forwarded to Gregg even though General Pleasonton seems to have missed the significance of the report.[12] As a result, Gregg knew Stuart was coming even before he arrived. If Stuart's mission was so hush-hush, the planning for the secret mission was atrocious because it did not account for the easy detection of the movement of a large body of cavalry on a hot dry day. The only rational explanation is that Stuart's primary mission was just as he and Lee reported: to operate on the Confederate right and protect Ewell's flank.

11 Ibid., 245.

12 *OR* 27, pt. 1, 956.

The fight at Brinkerhoff's Ridge revealed a large force of Union cavalry operating on the Union right flank (the Army of Northern Virginia's far left flank). Until Brig. Gen. Wesley Merritt's Reserve Brigade arrived from Emmitsburg, Maryland, about 11:00 a.m. on July 3, there had been no Union cavalry operating on the Confederate right flank since the withdrawal of John Buford's division 24 hours earlier.[13] Hence, there was no significant threat to Lee's right from Union cavalry and no reason to position Stuart's command there as a blocking force.

While the fighting was underway at Brinkerhoff's Ridge on July 2, Wade Hampton's Southern cavalry brigade was tangling with Judson Kilpatrick's division at Hunterstown, several miles north of the Confederate left flank. From this position Kilpatrick's division, if left unopposed, could have easily swept around the Army of Northern Virginia's left flank and into its unguarded rear.[14] The presence of a division-sized force of Union cavalry that far from the main body of the Army of the Potomac was perceived as another attempt to turn Lee's flank.[15] That two full divisions of cavalry—four brigades, or fully half of the eight brigades of cavalry assigned to the

13 Carhart is wrong when he claims Meade was too cautious to order operations along the flanks. It should be pointed out that using cavalry to secure an army's flanks and to harass the enemy's flanks is a classic role for the mounted arm of an army. See, e.g., Napoleon's Maxim of War 50: "Charges of cavalry . . . should be made always, if possible, on the flanks of the infantry, especially when the latter is engaged in front." Lieut. Gen. Sir G. G. D'Aguilar, C. B., trans., *Napoleon's Art of War* (New York: Barnes & Noble, 1995), 73. In fact, Judson Kilpatrick had explicit orders to operate on the Confederate far left, and was late arriving on the field only because Kilpatrick did not know where Custer's brigade was, and spent time searching for it. Merritt's brigade from Buford's First Division also had orders to operate on the Confederate far right. In addition, Gregg had specific orders to operate on the Confederate far left. See *OR* 27, pt. 1, 992 (Kilpatrick's report), 943 (Merritt's report), and 956 (Gregg's report). The reports of these three cavalry commanders contradict a fundamental aspect of Carhart's theory. I included a detailed discussion of Kilpatrick's and Merritt's operations along the Confederate far right flank in my book *Gettysburg's Forgotten Cavalry Actions: Farnsworth's Charge, South Cavalry Field, and the Battle of Fairfield, July 3, 1863* (El Dorado Hills, CA: Savas Beatie, 2012).

14 For a detailed discussion of the nasty fight at Hunterstown, see Wittenberg and Petruzzi, *Plenty of Blame to Go Around*, 161-177.

15 When Wade Hampton wrote his report of the action at Hunterstown, he stated: "The brigade was stationed on July 2, at Hunterstown, 5 miles to the east of Gettysburg, when orders came from General Stuart that it should move up, and take position on the left of our infantry. Before this could be accomplished, I was notified that a large force of cavalry was advancing on Hunterstown, with a view to get in the rear of our army. Communicating this information to General Stuart, I was ordered by him to return, and hold the enemy in check." *OR* 27, pt. 2, 724.

Army of the Potomac's Cavalry Corps—were operating simultaneously on or near his left flank justifiably alarmed Lee. Would the Federals make a concerted effort to turn his flank with two divisions of cavalry on July 3? It is therefore no surprise that Lee would want Jeb Stuart to guard that flank. That is why Stuart's four brigades of veteran cavalry (roughly the size of the Union force known to have been operating on the Confederate left) were there on July 3. Putting Stuart and his weary troopers on that flank is the only disposition that makes any sense, and one that comports with the reports filed by both Lee and Stuart.

Carhart's theory doesn't even account for the presence of John Gregg's Union brigade, or the fact that it could have checked any attempt by Stuart to dash down the Low Dutch Road. Even if Stuart managed to brush McIntosh and Custer aside and head for the Union rear via the Low Dutch Road, David Gregg had planned for that contingency. By keeping his cousin John Gregg's brigade in reserve, Gregg had 1,500-2,000 veteran horse soldiers available to pitch into Stuart's flank and make any attempted ride down the Low Dutch Road a miserable experience, hindering Stuart's progress while the rest of Gregg's command rallied and pitched back into the fight.[16] As David Gregg himself put it, "Had General Stuart attempted to pass between our position & Gettysburg, to accomplish his surprise, this 2nd Brigade would have fastened on his flank and held him until joined by the others."[17] This was good planning by a capable veteran commander, and it paid dividends.

Finally, the presence of Stuart's command on the Confederate far left freed James Walker's Stonewall Brigade from having to hold Brinkerhoff's Ridge, and relieved William "Extra Billy" Smith's brigade (Early's division) from picket duty.[18] This, in turn, allowed Ewell to assign Smith to Edward Johnson's division so that Johnson could commit two additional brigades of veteran Virginians against Culp's Hill on July 3. The attacks the

16 In an 1884 letter to John B. Bachelder, Irvin Gregg stated that his brigade mustered between 1,600-2,000 sabers on July 3, 1863. Ladd and Ladd, *Bachelder's History*, 761.

17 Gregg, "The Second Cavalry Division of the Army of the Potomac in the Gettysburg Campaign," 14.

18 As noted, Col. William A. Morgan of the 1st Virginia Cavalry of Fitz Lee's brigade remembered that as his brigade came on the field, it specifically linked up with the 2nd Virginia Infantry of the Stonewall Brigade, thereby extending the Confederate infantry's line of battle and covering the left flank. Morgan, "Desperate Charges."

previous night had nearly carried the rocky heights; another 2,100 veteran Virginians might allow Johnson's renewed assault to carry the day.

There are other problems with Carhart's theory. First, it fails to account for the wretched condition of Stuart's command after its brutal eight-day ride to Gettysburg. At most, Stuart fielded perhaps 2,500 effective troopers on serviceable mounts, not the 6,000 claimed by Carhart.[19] Carhart also greatly overstates the strength of Witcher's command, which he claims numbered 1,000. Witcher's own account puts the number at about 550.[20]

Second, I believe Carhart fails to account for the terrain. Any attacks against Culp's Hill would have been across the worst ground imaginable for cavalry operations—terrain described by Confederate staff officer Henry Kyd Douglas as "that second Devil's Den." No cavalry commander would have considered operating on that ground, especially one as capable as Jeb Stuart.[21] Witcher himself had little experience commanding his men in combat (to date they had performed primarily partisan ranger duties). Finally, Witcher's small and largely inexperienced command would not have been able to drive entrenched veteran Union infantry from Culp's Hill. To suggest that these undisciplined and unreliable men could have done so is in my opinion simply not credible.

Carhart also states: "Lee would give Stuart command of his only other cavalry unit, Jenkins' brigade of some 1,000 mounted riflemen."[22] Calling Jenkins' brigade the only other available cavalry unit attached to the Army of Northern Virginia on the morning of July 3 is demonstrably wrong. Brig. Gen. John D. Imboden's brigade (the Northwestern Brigade) arrived on the battlefield by noon on July 3. As Imboden put it, "I reported direct to General Lee for orders, and was assigned a position to aid in repelling any cavalry demonstration on his rear."[23] Not only were additional cavalry forces

19 Busey and Martin, *Regimental Strengths and Losses*, 196-199. As Stuart himself wrote, "some regiments were reduced to less than 100 men" by the time they arrived at Gettysburg. *OR* 27, pt. 2, 709.

20 Witcher, "Chambersburg Raid."

21 Douglas, *I Rode with Stonewall*, 249.

22 Carhart, *Lost Triumph*, 159.

23 John D. Imboden, "The Confederate Retreat from Gettysburg," in Robert U. Johnson and Clarence C. Buel, eds. *Battles and Leaders of the Civil War*, 4 vols. (New York: The Century Co. 1888), 3:420.

available to Lee, but the general remained concerned that a sortie into his rear was a real possibility—even though he had sent Stuart's command to his far left in order to checkmate any such thrust. In addition to Imboden, cavalry brigades under Brig. Gen. Beverly H. Robertson (two very large regiments of mostly inexperienced North Carolina cavalry) and Brig. Gen. William E. "Grumble" Jones (three regiments of excellent veteran Virginia horse soldiers from the Shenandoah Valley who had borne the brunt of the fighting at Brandy Station and at Upperville on the way north) arrived in the Cashtown area five miles behind the main Confederate line of battle during the morning of July 3. They were available to ride to the main battlefield if needed. Instead, Lee ordered these two brigades to operate near Fairfield, Pennsylvania, to secure the Jack's Mountain passes and keep Lee's line of retreat open.[24]

Carhart's claim that the four shots fired by Stuart's artillery at the start of the engagement were intended to announce to Lee that Stuart's command was in place is also unsupportable. Here is what Carhart writes about this issue:

> Lee would have told Stuart to get his men ready to move out to Cress Ridge, that he would give him the final signal to leave at the right time. Stuart would have been very easily able to move three or so miles on the York Pike and then down another mile into the woods atop Cress Ridge, a site Stuart had no doubt visited the day before with Fitz Lee and probably (as any good commander would have made sure to do) Hampton and Chambliss as well. Hampton and Fitz Lee's brigades were already out north of the York Pike, in good position to move down onto Cress Ridge, while Stuart had spent the night in town with the brigades of Chambliss and Jenkins. Lee would give him the word to begin moving those brigades and send couriers to alert the others well before he started his artillery barrage. Once Stuart had assembled his four brigades on Cress Ridge, he should keep them well concealed in the woods and signal to Lee by cannon shots that he had arrived what his prospects where. This signal would give Lee important information on which the development of the rest of his battle plan would depend.

24 *OR* 27, pt. 2, 752.

The signals agreed upon are open to conjecture, but we can say some things about the code that must have been involved. One shot would have meant nothing, for a single cannon being fired near an active battlefield could too easily have been fired by someone else and would mean nothing. The same might be true for two shots, or they might be a peremptory signal, like the simple fact that the York Pike was blocked or for some other reason Stuart could not make it to the top of Cress Ridge. Three shots would mean that Stuart had arrived at Cress Ridge, but is path to Bonaughton Road was barred by a strong Union force that seemed capable of keeping him from reaching it. And four shots would mean that he had arrived on Cress Ridge and the way was clear before him, that there was nothing apparent that might slow him down as he moved his men down the valley and headed them south on Bonaughton Road.

That last signal could be the best possible outcome, for it meant that from Cress Ridge Stuart had to move about one mile down to the junction of the Hanover Road and Bonaughton Road, another mile down Bonaughton Road to the Baltimore Pike, and then perhaps three-quarters of a mile up Baltimore Pike to the rear of Culp's Hill. That was a total of less than three miles, and Stuart's cavalry could cover that distance at a trot in less than twenty minutes. Stuart would then save his horses over that stretch, for once he got behind Culp's Hill and Jenkins' brigade dismounted and reassumed their infantry role, the rest of his men would have dug in their spurs. They then would have descended like apocalyptic banshees on the back side of the Clump of Trees and Cemetery Hill, a fury of death and destruction striking the Union soldiers in the rear while their anxious attention would be riveted on Pickett's Charge to their front.

If Stuart reached Cress Ridge, found the way clear, and fired four shots, Lee would proceed with the rest of his attack. He planned to fire his artillery against Union gun emplacements and infantry positions behind the Clump of Trees, a bombardment that would last for more than an hour, perhaps as much as two hours. But he would not open fire until he had heard Stuart's signal. If he heard four shots, he would launch the attack. If Stuart's signal was something else, that would mean he could probably not get through and Lee would have to consider other actions.[25]

Once again, and as Carhart reluctantly admits, there is no objective evidence to support this theory. There is no proof Stuart moved any farther east than Brinkerhoff's Ridge on July 2, and there is no evidence to suggest Fitz Lee rode anywhere with him that night. Hampton could not have accompanied Stuart because his command did not shake itself loose from the Hunterstown engagement until about 6:30 p.m. on July 2. (Hampton could not have reached Gettysburg before 7:15 or 7:30 p.m., and he had the cumbersome wagon train to worry about.) Stuart and his lieutenants were nowhere near Cress Ridge on the night of July 2.

Carhart's theory also ignores the intense infantry fight that raged on Culp's Hill on the morning of July 3 between elements of the Union I Corps and XII Corps and Ewell's Second Corps. The Union troops launched a spoiling attack and thereafter Edward Johnson's Confederate division engaged in several assaults, all of which were repulsed. The fighting was over by noon, when the Confederates bloodily beat back an ill-advised counterattack by two Union regiments.[26] By the time the guns fell silent on Culp's Hill, however, Stuart had already fired the four artillery shots on Cress Ridge. There was also skirmishing along the main line of battle prior to the bombardment preceding Pickett's Charge. Simply put, under these circumstances it would have been impossible for Lee to hear four cannon shots from nearly seven miles away.

Finally, Carhart's theory does not take into account reloading the gun. It is clear that only a single artillery piece was employed. That gun had to be reloaded three times in order to fire four shots.[27] In 1860, General John

25 Carhart, *Lost Triumph*, 177-178.

26 Obviously, a detailed discussion of the fighting for Culp's Hill strays far beyond the scope of this essay. For more information on this subject, see Pfanz, *Culp's Hill*, 310-353.

27 Each gun was manned by seven enlisted men, labeled numbers one through seven, and was typically commanded by a sergeant. A section consisted of two guns, and was typically commanded by a lieutenant. Confederate batteries had two sections, with a captain as the battery commander. The following is the routine followed by a gun crew to load and fire a muzzle-loading Civil War cannon such as those used by Stuart's horse artillery: 1. Position or move the gun, particularly after the recoil induced by firing the gun. 2. Number one sponged the gun barrel and rammed home the next charge. 3. Number two received the

Gibbon wrote an artillery manual for the United States Army. It was the standard manual for field artillery for both sides in 1863. According to Gibbon, "Generally, the rate of fire should be much less than one shot per minute."[28] Indeed the rate of fire varied. "The rate of fire depended upon a number of circumstances. Generally speaking, a gun could fire two solid shot, shell, or spherical case rounds in one minute; or three rounds of canister in one minute," notes artillery historian George Newton, a Licensed Battlefield Guide at Gettysburg. "Canister did not require the time to reset the gun and aim, as did the other longer range projectiles, because it was nothing more than a large shotgun blast."[29] In the present case, the gun was fired in four different directions, meaning the gun would not only have to be reloaded each time, but repositioned each time. It is highly unlikely Stuart would have wasted canister (which was only effective at very short range of 100-200 yards) in such a scenario, so it would have taken longer to reload. Therefore, the shots were at least sixty seconds apart and maybe as much as 90 seconds or more. Regardless, firing four shots from a single gun would not have made for a very effective signal.

By contrast, the Confederates utilized two signal guns to commence the grand cannonade prior to the Pickett-Pettigrew-Trimble charge. The Army of Northern Virginia had 140 guns ready to bombard the Union line. When the time came to begin the cannonade, two guns were run forward to a

---

charge from number five, powder cartridge in right hand and shot in left and loaded these into the muzzle of the gun. 4. While the gun was being loaded, number three covered the vent hole with a thumb stall to prevent a draft of air that could cause a premature explosion of the black powder charge, and after the gun was loaded, he pierced the powder cartridge by inserting the primer wire through the vent hole. 5. Number four inserted the lanyard into the hole of the friction primer, to drop the primer tube into the vent on the command "Ready", and to pull the lanyard to fire the gun. 6. At the command "Load," number five ran to the ammunition chest, received the cartridge and projectile from number six or seven, who shared the task of preparing and issuing the ammunition under the supervision of the chief of caisson, and carried them to number two. John W. Rowell, *Yankee Artillerymen: Through the Civil War with Eli Lilly's Indiana Battery* (Knoxville: University of Tennessee Press, 1975), 29.

28 John Gibbon, *The Artillerist's Manual, Compiled from Various Sources and Adapted to the Service of the United States* (New York: D. Van Nostrand, 1860), 404. As Gibbon pointed out, if the rate of fire was more than one per minute, "the whole supply of a six-pounder being about 400 shots, if the firing was at the rate of one per minute, the whole provision for a campaign would be consumed in about seven hours." Ibid.

29 George Newton, *Silent Sentinels: A Reference Guide to the Artillery at Gettysburg* (New York: Savas Beatie, 2005), 60, 62.

conspicuous position and fired two shots. The first shot went as planned, and the second was to follow immediately. Because the friction primer failed, there was a gap of a few seconds for a new one to be inserted, and then the second shot rang out, followed by 138 other guns firing more or less in unison.[30] Those signal guns were only a few seconds apart and did not require reloading in order to complete the signal. They represent a true and appropriate use of signal guns, not what transpired on Cress Ridge. Indeed, if Stuart's shots on Cress Ridge were intended to be signal shots, wouldn't it have made much better sense to line up an entire battery of four guns and fire them consecutively, one right after another, so that the four shots were sequenced a second or two apart, instead of as much as 90 seconds apart? Carhart's theory does not allow for the reloading or repositioning of the guns, and makes it even more improbable.

So, with that in mind, what was the purpose of those artillery shots? The answer is actually rather simple. To use modern military parlance, the firing of those shots constituted a "reconnaissance by fire." Modern military doctrine defines it this way: "Reconnaissance by fire is accomplished by firing on likely or suspected enemy positions in an attempt to remove camouflage and to cause the enemy to disclose his presence by movement or return fire. During reconnaissance by fire, positions being reconnoitered must be observed continuously so enemy activity can be quickly and definitely located." If the enemy returns fire, the position is developed. If not, the fire continues until the enemy responds.[31]

It seems quite clear that this is precisely what Stuart intended. There is ample evidence in the historical record to support this contention. Years after the war, Alexander Pennington related a post-war conversation that he had with Stuart's adjutant, Maj. Henry B. McClellan. McClellan said "that Stuart looked in every direction but could find no sign of our troops, so he ordered a gun out and ordered it to be fired in different directions in hopes of getting an echo or a reply from one of our guns, and then through his glass locate the

---

30 Bradley M. Gottfried, *The Artillery of Gettysburg* (Nashville, TN: Cumberland House, 2008), 195.

31 U.S. Army Skill Level Guide 071-326-5805 (SL3), "Conduct a Route Reconnaissance Mission," www.armystudyguide.com/content/smct_ctt_tasks/skill_levels_2_4/07/13265 805-sl3-conduct-a-.shtml. It is also possible that Stuart was trying to signal Hampton and Chambliss, who were lagging behind, that the rest of the command was in position. That seems less likely, but it is plausible.

smoke."[32] This is the very definition of a reconnaissance by fire. McClellan continued: "He fired in one direction—no reply. He fired in another direction—no reply. Then in another direction, and then an answering gun. He said the shot from that gun entered the muzzle of their gun, and knocked it off the trunions, breaking two wheels."[33]

Given Stuart's dispositions—dismounting Chambliss and Witcher in the vicinity of the Rummel farm buildings, and then hiding the mounted brigades of Hampton and Fitz Lee in the woods—it appears obvious that he intended to skirmish with, and then ambush, David Gregg. The artillery shots were to announce his presence and develop Gregg's position, and to lure him into attacking Chambliss and Witcher. Once the Federals were engaged with Chambliss and Witcher, Stuart would unleash a mounted attack by Lee and Hampton, which would drive the blue clad horsemen right into the muzzles of the Confederate artillery and Chambliss and Witcher. In other words, Lee and Hampton would be the hammer, and the artillery and Chambliss and Witcher the anvil. Then, having defeated Gregg, he would then sortie down the Low Dutch Road to make some mischief in the Union rear.

In conclusion, the only logical explanation for his firing of the four shots was that Stuart waited until his troopers were in position, and then announced his presence to set his plan into motion. The artillery shots were a reconnaissance by fire, intended jointly to identify the position of Gregg's division and to entice Gregg into attacking. It really is that simple.

One other point should be made. Given that Cress Ridge is, as the crow flies, about seven miles from Lee's headquarters on Seminary Ridge, using signal guns would have been wholly ineffective. As pointed out above, the likelihood of those guns being distinctly heard over the din of battle seems quite unlikely and defies the laws of physics. Another option existed. Lieutenant Colonel Edward Porter Alexander, acting chief of artillery for Longstreet's Corps, had begun his army career as a signal officer, and he had helped to organize the Confederate Signal Corps in the early days of the Confederacy. He developed an effective system that included the use of signal rockets, which were used effectively by the Confederate armies as

---

32 Styple, *Generals in Bronze*, 259.

33 Ibid.

early as the July 1861 Battle of Bull Run.[34] Further, signal rockets were standard equipment to be carried in artillery limbers, meaning that Stuart would have had them available to use in order to let Lee know that he was in position and ready to move (if we accept the theory of signaling).[35] Or, as another alternative, the Confederate Signal Corps was also adept at semaphore by that stage of the war, and a Confederate signal officer could have wig-wagged to Lee from some identifiable height that Stuart was in position and ready to attack. The likelihood of the four cannon shots being signals to Lee, as claimed by Carhart, seems quite remote indeed, given the existence of other, more effective means of communication.

Stuart, ever the opportunist, would have availed himself of the opportunity to make mischief if it had availed itself, but that was not his primary mission. His primary mission was to secure Ewell's flank and prevent Gregg from turning that flank and getting into Lee's rear. His secondary mission was to ambush and defeat Gregg. Then, and only then, would Stuart sortie into the Union rear. Any other conclusion is unsupported by the historical record and/or defies common sense. Carhart's theories simply do not hold up under scrutiny.[36]

34 For a detailed discussion of the operations of the Confederate Signal Corps, see Edmund H. Cummins, "The Signal Corps in the Confederate States Army," *Southern Historical Society Papers*, 16 (1888), 93-107. Cummins specifically mentions the use of signal rockets by Confederate General P. G. T. Beauregard at the Battle of Bull Run, so this was a viable option.

35 Gibbon, *The Artillerist's Manual*, 376.

36 There are many other aspects of Carhart's theory that can be deeply critiqued. However, many are small details and so go beyond the scope of this appendix.

Appendix D

Which Confederate Battery Fired the Four Shots on Cress Ridge to Open the Fighting on East Cavalry Field?

Closely associated with the controversy over the purpose for the firing of four shots by Confederate horse artillery on Cress Ridge is the question of which of three Confederate horse artillery batteries might have fired those four random shots. Although not as well known, the controversy over which battery fired those four shots is just as enduring, and like its associated controversy, we will probably never know the right answer. Further complicating matters is the fact that none of the battery commanders—or any of their men—left behind a report or an account wherein the firing of the four random shots was even mentioned. Hence, it is all guesswork, although logic and a little good detective work can be used to exclude two of the three potential candidates.

There are three primary candidates, and each one has been cited in well-known histories as the source of those shots. The most frequently cited battery is Capt. Wiley Hunter Griffin's Second Maryland Artillery, which was also known as the Baltimore Light Artillery. Griffin was a Virginian who served with the Baltimore Light Artillery throughout the war. Griffin's battery was armed with four 10-pounder Parrott rifled guns, organized into two sections of two guns each.[1] In April 1863, the Baltimore Light Artillery

1 Newton, *Silent Sentinels*, 144.

was converted to horse artillery and assigned to Stuart's Horse Artillery. It accompanied Brig. Gen. Albert G. Jenkins' brigade during the invasion of Pennsylvania, and arrived on the Gettysburg battlefield on July 2.[2]

Stuart's reliable adjutant, Maj. Henry B. McClellan, left behind the best-known account of the fighting on East Cavalry Field in his memoirs, *The Life and Campaigns of Major-General J.E.B. Stuart.* McClellan wrote, "While carefully concealing Jenkins' and Chambliss' brigades from view, Stuart pushed one of Griffin's guns to the edge of the woods and fired a number of random shots in different directions, himself giving orders to the gun."[3] Because McClellan's memoirs are quite reliable and generally quite accurate, many historians give credence to this version of events and credit Griffin's battery with firing these shots.

However, McClellan eventually admitted to John B. Bachelder (the famous early Gettysburg battle historian) that he had made a mistake, and misidentified Griffin's battery for another.[4] Indeed he had. Griffin's battery was not on East Cavalry Field during the fighting there on July 3, 1863. William W. Goldsborough, who chronicled the exploits of Maryland Confederates, remembered that Maj. Joseph Latimer deployed Griffin's guns "a short distance to the left on the Cashtown pike. In the terrible battle that ensued, the Baltimore Light Artillery played its part."[5] The National Park Service construed this to mean that Griffin's battery was deployed on or near Oak Hill (near the modern-day Peace Light Memorial) and that it engaged in the heavy fighting for that important position.[6]

Historian Robert J. Trout, the modern authority on the Stuart Horse Artillery, has done an analysis of this question, and determined that Griffin's battery was actually deployed near Benner's Hill not far from Rock Creek,

---

2 W. W. Goldsborough, *The Maryland Line in the Confederate Army* (Baltimore: Guggenheimer, Weil & Co., 1900), 275-284.

3 McClellan, *The Life and Campaigns*, 338.

4 McClellan to Bachelder, May 17, 1886, *The Bachelder Papers*, 3:1,384-1,385. McClellan wrote: "It now seems clear *Jackson's* battery near Trostle's and the *Louisiana section* near Rummel's were *the only artillery* employed by the Confederates in the early part of the fight (emphasis added)."

5 Goldsborough, *The Maryland Line*, 285.

6 The National Park Service's unit markers show Griffin's battery deployed on Oak Hill, and many other sources have picked up on this error.

nowhere near either Oak Ridge or Cress Ridge. Latimer's battalion was instead blasted off of Benner's Hill by Union artillery on July 2 when Latimer was killed, and the gunners were never deployed on Oak Hill. It appears that Goldsborough misidentified the Cashtown Road. A review of a map of the wartime road network in Gettysburg shows that the Cashtown Road passed through the town and continued to the east as it does today. It then splits. Part becomes the York Pike and part becomes the Hanover Road. The likelihood is that Griffin's guns were deployed a short distance out on either the York Pike or the Hanover Road, east of the town of Gettysburg, and near Lt. Gen. Richard S. Ewell's headquarters which was in the Y created by the two roads. Finally, it appears that the Baltimore Light Artillery was confused for Capt. Abraham Hupp's Salem Artillery, commanded by Lt. Charles B. Griffin. The Salem Artillery was deployed on Seminary Ridge north of the Cashtown Road, and participated in the grand cannonade preceding the Pickett-Pettigrew-Trimble attack. It is, therefore, clear that Wiley Griffin's Baltimore Light Artillery was nowhere near Cress Ridge and could not have fired the shots that opened the ball on East Cavalry Field.[7]

In his critically acclaimed book *Gettysburg: Day Three*, historian Jeffry D. Wert claims the two guns of Capt. Charles A. Green's Louisiana Guard Artillery (temporarily attached to Stuart's command on July 2 and 3) fired the shots, as he did again in his excellent 2009 biography of Jeb Stuart. Wert appears to be the only major historian to claim that Green's guns fired these shots. Green's section of two ten-pounder Parrotts was temporarily attached to Hampton's brigade to assist in the repulse of Custer's Wolverines at Hunterstown late on the afternoon of July 2. The Louisiana Guard Artillery was normally part of Lt. Col. Hilary P. Jones' artillery battalion, which served with Maj. Gen. Jubal A. Early's Second Corps division. Consequently, it was not a horse artillery unit, and its complement of men either walked behind the guns, or rode on the limbers and caissons as horses pulled them from place to place.[8] By definition, Green's guns could not have

7 Trout, *Galloping Thunder*, 654-658.

8 Wert, *Gettysburg: Day Three*, 261; Wert, *Cavalryman of the Lost Cause*, 286. These types of units were referred to as "mounted artillery." John Gibbon explained its meaning, that "the cannoneers are on foot, and remain so during the maneuvers of the battery, except when it is desired to move at a very rapid rate, when they are mounted on the ammunition

kept up with Hampton's cavalry, and would have arrived on Cress Ridge sometime after Hampton's brigade. By the time that Green arrived on Cress Ridge, it is quite likely that the four shots would already have been fired.

The source of this confusion is understandable. When he penned his report, Captain Green wrote that his two guns "moved forward with General Hampton's cavalry through the town of Hunterstown, and turning to the right, reached a position some 3 miles distant from the left of our lines, where, with a brigade of General Stuart's cavalry, we encountered a large cavalry force of the enemy, with a battery of six pieces of artillery." According to Green, the engagement began about 2:00, with dismounted skirmishers opening the action. "My two guns were placed in position, and opened on their sharpshooters and a column of cavalry advancing. My shells exploded well, and seemed to have the desired effect on the enemy. Their guns now commenced a severe fire on my section and the cavalry fight becoming general, I was ordered to cease firing and withdraw my pieces."[9]

A close examination of Green's report indicates that his two guns could not have fired the four shots that opened the ball. Green clearly says that when his guns unlimbered and opened fire, dismounted sharpshooters were already engaged. This can only be the dismounted advance of the 5th Michigan Cavalry against Witcher's position at the Rummel farm, meaning that the fighting was already well underway by the time that Green arrived and opened fire. Since the four shots opened the action, there is no way that Green's guns could have fired them under any circumstances.

Hampton's report confirms this conclusion. When he penned his report of the campaign after recuperating from his Gettysburg wounds, Hampton recounted that after his brigade arrived at Cress Ridge, he "took position on the left of Colonel Chambliss, and threw out sharpshooters to check an advance the enemy were attempting. Soon after, General Fitz Lee came up, and took position on my left. The sharpshooters soon became actively engaged, and succeeded perfectly in keeping the enemy back, while the three brigades were held ready to meet any charge made by the enemy. We had for the three brigades but two pieces of artillery, while the enemy had apparently

---

boxes." Gibbon, *The Artillerist's Manual*, 388. By contrast, in the horse artillery each man assigned to serve with the battery had his own horse that he used to move from place to place, enabling them to keep up with the quick-moving cavalry.

9 *OR* 27, pt. 2, 497.

two batteries in position." Hampton's account confirms that the Confederate horse artillery that opened the battle had already been blasted off Cress Ridge by the deadly fire of Pennington's guns by the time that Green's two guns arrived, meaning that the engagement was already well under way. Accordingly, it is impossible for Green's guns to have fired those first shots at the opening of the engagement on Cress Ridge.[10]

Having eliminated both Griffin's and Green's batteries, only the horse artillery battery of Capt. Thomas E. Jackson remains as the source of the four shots. Additional information supports this conclusion. In a letter to his father, Lt. Micajah Woods, a commander of a section of Jackson's battery, described the damage his guns suffered from Pennington's guns:

> The first shell thrown burst about 40 feet from me—covering me with dirt and a fragment grazed my leg about two inches below my knee, cut my pants and passed on—only bruising the flesh, but scarcely scratching it enough to draw blood. We stood before them about ten minutes when Maj. Terrell commander of our Battalion ordered the pieces from the field. In that time four of the horses at the gun I had taken in especial charge had been killed & several had been wounded in my section. Several spokes had been cut by the balls & shells & my carriages were being so injured I could scarcely get them off the field.[11]

Lieutenant Woods' description matches Pennington's of the damage inflicted by his fire. Pennington claimed his first shots not only disabled a gun, but also broke two wheels of Woods' two guns.[12] Since the descriptions match, and there is no other account of a Confederate battery suffering the type of damage described by both Federal officers, it seems clear that the battery in question was Jackson's, and not Griffin's (which was not even present on Cress Ridge) or Green's (which had not yet arrived on the field).

Hopefully, this particular controversy has finally been put to rest, and the Confederate battery that fired the opening shots of the East Cavalry Field battle has been satisfactorily identified.

---

10 Ibid., 724.

11 Trout, *Galloping Thunder*, 293.

12 Styple, *Generals in Bronze*, 259.

Driving Tour: The Battles for
Brinkerhoff's Ridge and East Cavalry Field

Now that you are familiar with the tactical details of the fights for Brinkerhoff's Ridge and East Cavalry Field, you are ready to take a driving tour of these sites that are just outside the main Gettysburg battlefield. It is chronologically important to see the Brinkerhoff's Ridge battlefield first, but you will see two important sites from the battle at Brinkerhoff's Ridge after you complete the East Cavalry Field tour. The tour includes GPS coordinates for all of the pertinent sites. Note that photographs (taken by the author) of the important landmarks and monuments from the fights for Brinkerhoff's Ridge and East Cavalry Field are scattered throughout the text of this driving tour to assist you in identifying all locations. Take your time. Study these relatively pristine battlefields to appreciate what the men of both sides saw during the battles. And above all, enjoy!

The Tour Begins

Depart from the Gettysburg National Military Park Museum and Visitor Center via the Baltimore Pike (GPS BENCHMARK 1). Turn left onto the Baltimore Pike (GPS BENCHMARK 2). Travel 1.4 miles north (it becomes Baltimore Street) to the town square (GPS BENCHMARK 3). At the square, turn right onto U.S. Route 30 (York Street, which later becomes the York Pike). Continue for .2 miles until you come to a Y in the road (GPS

BENCHMARK 4). Take the right fork of the Y, which is the Hanover Road (Pa. State Route 116).

To Brinkerhoff's Ridge

Continue east on the Hanover Road for 2.3 miles. You will pass Benner's Hill, which was an important Confederate artillery position during the attacks on Culp's Hill. Stop if you like, as it's an important spot that does not get a great deal of visitation. Just beyond Benner's Hill, on the left side of the road, you will see the stone Daniel Lady farmhouse and barn. These buildings, which have recently been restored, were there at the time of the battle. When you have traveled 2.1 miles from the intersection of the Hanover and York roads, you will see the monument to the 10th New York Cavalry on your left (GPS BENCHMARK 5). It sits on the south slope of Brinkerhoff's Ridge. Be very careful here as this is a busy road with swiftly moving traffic. If you are safely able, feel free to stop and look at the monument, but remember that it is on private property. Continue another .2 miles and turn left onto Hoffman Road (GPS BENCHMARK 6). As you make the turn, you will see a War Department marker for the Brinkerhoff's Ridge fight on your left. Continue .1 of a mile and turn left into the driveway for the electrical power station (GPS BENCHMARK 7). Park your car and get out, but be aware that this is an active power station on private property, so please conduct yourself accordingly and do not block access to the station.

The Brinkerhoff's Ridge Battlefield

Cross Hoffman Road. Unfortunately, the stone wall that lined the eastern side of the road that became the focus of the fighting for Brinkerhoff's Ridge was obliterated by the property owner in 2008. Standing here, you are on the position held by the 3rd Pennsylvania Cavalry. The Pennsylvanians held the other side of the wall, facing you. The Confederate position is behind you, atop the ridge, but with the men of the 2nd Virginia Infantry advancing down the ridge toward you. If the foliage is not too high and you look to the northeast, you should be able to see the

10th New York Cavalry Monument.

Author

Michigan Cavalry Brigade monument and the Cavalry Shaft in the distance on the East Cavalry Field.

You will also see Cress Ridge rising in front of you. If you look off to your right, across the Hanover Road (Pa. Route 116), you will notice a farm with a large barn and some exotic animals. This farm occupies that portion of the battlefield held by the 1st New Jersey Cavalry and the single company of the Purnell Legion. This is private property, and you should not enter onto the land without permission. As you look in front of you, the low ground and house in front is the valley created by Cress Run. The house along its banks is the John Cress house. You will get a better view of the Cress house and the Abraham Reever house as you return from the East Cavalry Field part of the tour. Be sure to note the lay of the land. As you do, your vantage point will closely approximate the one held by Jeb Stuart late in the afternoon of July 2, 1863.

Recall that the fighting for Brinkerhoff's Ridge is important to set the stage for the fighting that occurred on East Cavalry Field the next day. The stone wall served as the demarcation line between the Union and Confederate forces, and was the focus of the fighting. Gregg's dismounted troopers attacked the wall from the east, while the men of the 2nd Virginia Infantry defended from the west. The Union attacks were perpendicular to the Hanover Road, and on either side of the Hanover Road. Gregg's troopers finally secured the stone wall and drove the Virginia infantrymen back to the crest of Brinkerhoff's Ridge. Jeb Stuart watched the climax of the fighting from the highest point of the ridge, above the power station, where he could also see Cress Ridge and portions of East Cavalry Field in the distance. He also realized that an entire division of veteran Union infantry was operating on the Army of Northern Virginia's far left flank in addition to the engagement between Judson Kilpatrick's Third Cavalry Division and Hampton's Brigade of Stuart's command at Hunterstown, to the north and east of Brinkerhoff's Ridge, meaning that Stuart knew that four full brigades of Union cavalry were in a position to threaten the Army of Northern Virginia's left flank and rear.

The Route to East Cavalry Field

Return to your car and turn left as you emerge from the driveway of the electrical power station. Continue north on Hoffman Road for 1.5 miles. As you proceed along Hoffman Road, look to your right. You will have a good view of the commanding high ground offered by the heavily wooded Cress Ridge.

After traveling 1.5 miles, you will come to the intersection of Hoffman Road and Cavalry Field Road (GPS BENCHMARK 8). Turn right onto Cavalry Field Road. Proceed along Cavalry Field Road for .2 miles. On your left, you will find the Isaac Miller farm, which was a Confederate field hospital for wounded from the East Cavalry Field fighting. Proceed another

The view from Cress Ridge.

Author

.2 miles. Where the road becomes narrow you have entered onto National Park Service property. This narrow road, which tracks the original road trace taken by the Confederate cavalry on the morning of July 3, 1863, should give you a good idea of what a Civil War era road would have looked like. Where the road curves to the right and becomes the paved park road, please note that the original road trace continues into the heavy stand of woods directly ahead of you. That dirt road continues on into the woods toward the Low Dutch Road and was taken by Wade Hampton's and Fitzhugh Lee's brigades as they filtered onto the East Cavalry Field. Take the curve to the right and park in the pullover (GPS BENCHMARK 9) along Confederate Cavalry Avenue. You have entered and are viewing East Cavalry Field from the Confederate perspective.

The Opening Guns

Walk over to the artillery pieces parked along Confederate Cavalry Avenue. Remember that Confederate Avenue was not here at the time of the battle. Instead, a stout stone wall lined the farm fields and ran along the route of the modern-day Park Service road. Be sure to stand where you can see the entire field. Again, please note the lay of the land—your position on Cress Ridge is the highest point in the area. Also note that because of the lay of the land, you cannot see what lies at the bottom of the ridge.

This spot was Jeb Stuart's headquarters for most of the afternoon of July 3. It also marks the spot where Stuart deployed Jackson's battery and fired the day's opening shots. Note the terrain. If you are at the top of Cress Ridge, at Stuart's headquarters, you cannot see the Rummel farm buildings. After finishing your survey of the terrain in front of you, return to your car. The guns further down the ridge represent the two Napoleons of Green's battery serving with Stuart on East Cavalry Field.

The Rummel Farm

After you drive .4 of a mile down the slope of Cress Ridge, you will see the Rummel farm buildings in front of you on the left side of Confederate Cavalry Avenue (GPS BENCHMARK 10). The barn on your left is the Rummel barn, which was occupied by the men of Lt. Col. Vincent A. Witcher's 34th Battalion of Virginia Cavalry during the early dismounted portion of the battle. The house is not the wartime structure. The wartime

The Rummel barn.

Author

The Rummel farm as seen from the position of the 5th Michigan Cavalry.

Author

house stood to the left and front of the current house. The Rummel farm, while within the National Park Service's boundaries, is in private hands. The owners of the Rummel farm (as of this publication) are well aware of the historical significance of their property and love to show off the battle damage to the barn. However, please do not enter the barn without the permission of the owners of the property. If they are home when you visit, they may be willing to show you the damage to the Rummel barn. Where Confederate Cavalry Avenue curves to the left, you will see farm fields on either side of the road. The men of the 5th and 6th Michigan Cavalry regiments held those farm fields during the dismounted phase of the fighting for the Rummel farm and attacked toward the Rummel barn from two different directions, from your right and from directly in front of you. Return to your car and drive .5 of a mile to the pull over by the monument to the 1st New Jersey Cavalry (GPS BENCHMARK 11). Stop here and get out.

The 1st New Jersey Cavalry Monument.

Author

The Fight of the 1st New Jersey
and the 3rd Pennsylvania Cavalry

Be sure to read the wayside marker at the pullover. It will give you some additional interpretation of the fighting for the Rummel farm buildings. Also, be sure to read the text of the 1st New Jersey Cavalry's monument. The heavy casualties taken by the officer corps of the regiment will surprise you. One of the two original Rummel farm lanes lies to the right of the 1st New Jersey's monument and looks much as it would have in 1863. Dismounted Federals of the 1st New Jersey and 3rd Pennsylvania advanced part way down the farm lane in their attacks on the Rummel farm buildings. Little's Run lies to the right (west) of the Rummel farm lane, about 40 yards from the monument to the 1st New Jersey Cavalry. Be sure to obtain a full 360-degree perspective of this area in order to understand the importance of the terrain and the significance of this position. As you stand at the pullover and survey the Rummel farm buildings, remember that the present house was not there at the time of the battle. Also, be sure to look north toward the top of Cress Ridge where you made your first stop on the East Cavalry Field. Please note that you cannot see the position of Stuart's headquarters due to the lay of the land. This means that Stuart also could not see the fighting taking place on the grounds of the Rummel farm for the same reason. Be careful with the National Park Service wayside marker here—it inaccurately states that Stuart's objective was to exploit the anticipated success of the Confederate infantry assault on Cemetery Ridge. Return to your car.

The Brooke-Rawle Flagpole

Travel .1 of a mile and you will see a flagpole to the right of the road (GPS BENCHMARK 12). This is called the Brooke-Rawle Flag Pole, raised in tribute to Lt. William Brooke-Rawle of the 3rd Pennsylvania Cavalry, who spent much of his life documenting the fighting on the East Cavalry Field. Brooke-Rawle is the lowest-ranking officer to have a monument on the battlefield at Gettysburg. Continue on for another .2 of a mile to the next pullover at Custer Avenue (GPS BENCHMARK 13) which is actually just a grassy lane. Get out of your car here and be sure to read the wayside marker along Gregg Avenue.

The Brooke-Rawle flagpole.

Author

The Michigan Cavalry Brigade Monument

After you read the wayside marker at the head of Custer Avenue, be sure to get a panoramic view of the lay of the land. Please note that you cannot see the Rummel farm buildings as you look to your left, and you also cannot see the position of Stuart's headquarters atop Cress Ridge to your front. If you

The Michigan Cavalry Brigade Monument.

Author

look to your right, you will see the Lott farm buildings nearby and, in the distance, the silver metal roof of the barn at the intersection of the Hanover and Low Dutch roads.

Walk over to the Michigan Cavalry Brigade monument, and read its text. Instead of erecting separate monuments to each of the four regiments of the brigade, the State of Michigan elected to honor the entire brigade. Note the frieze of the charge of the 1st Michigan Cavalry on the front of the monument and the portrait of Custer above it. A typical Michigan cavalryman tops the monument. If you stand with your back to the monument, the charges of the 1st and 7th Michigan would have come from behind you, from the junction of the Hanover and Low Dutch roads. The charges would have overlapped you on both sides as they spread out across the fields.

Face the road and look to the left, and you will see a line of trees. This represents the position of the fence line that separated the 1st Virginia and 7th Michigan regiments during their fight. It is the same fence against which Wade Hampton was trapped and where he was wounded during the mounted melee. The Michigan Cavalry Brigade monument roughly marks where the 1st Michigan Cavalry crashed into Hampton's charging brigade. Return to your car, drive .1 of a mile, and park at the next pullover.

The Purnell Legion Monument.

Author

The Cavalry Shaft, the Monument to the Purnell Legion, and the Monument to the 3rd Pennsylvania Cavalry

Walk over to the Cavalry Shaft (GPS BENCHMARK 14), which is the obelisk surrounded by the wrought iron fence to your left. This monument was dedicated in 1884 to honor the horse soldiers of both the Union and the Confederacy that clashed on the East Cavalry Field. It is one of the few monuments on any Civil War battlefield to pay tribute to both sides.

The Cavalry Shaft.

Author

The 3rd Pennsylvania Cavalry Monument.

Author

Continue along the path to the monument to the 3rd Pennsylvania Cavalry, which marks the approximate location of Capt. William E. Miller's squadron and the starting point for Miller's heroic charge. As you stand by the monument and face north in the direction of the Rummel farm buildings, you will approximate the direction of Miller's charge. Be sure to get a panoramic view of the entire East Cavalry Field battlefield from the location of the 3rd Pennsylvania Cavalry's monument.

When you look north toward the Rummel farm buildings, you will also be able to see the length of McIntosh's position. McIntosh's line of battle extended from the strip of woods north of the Lott house to the fence near the Rummel Spring House, then toward the Hanover Road, following the meandering route of Little's Run. You will also see the monument to the single company of the Purnell Legion Cavalry assigned to Gregg's Division.

Return to your car. Drive .3 of a mile to the Low Dutch Road (GPS BENCHMARK 15). Along the way, you will pass the monument to the 1st Maryland Cavalry. Turn right onto the Low Dutch Road. Continue south on the Low Dutch Road for .1 of a mile, and then turn right onto the National Park Service Road (GPS BENCHMARK 16). The farm buildings in front of you are the buildings of the Lott farm, which were there during the battle.

The 1st Maryland Cavalry (U.S.) Monument.

Author

The Monuments to Randol's Battery

After traveling .2 of a mile, you will find the monument and guns of Chester's and then Woodruff's and Hamilton's sections of Capt. Alanson M. Randol's battery (GPS BENCHMARK 17). Stop and get out here. It is important to note that the guns were not actually positioned here, but were instead closer to the Low Dutch Road. Nevertheless, you will have an excellent perspective of the vista enjoyed by the Union horse artillerists. At the climax of the battle, elements of the grand Confederate charge nearly reached this position before the charge of the 1st Michigan Cavalry blunted them. Get back in your car and continue on for another .3 of a mile, where you will find the monument to the remaining section of Randol's battery (GPS BENCHMARK 18).

The Monument to Pennington's Battery and the Monument to the 1st Maine Cavalry

Travel another .1 of a mile and park near the monument and guns of Pennington's battery (GPS BENCHMARK 19). This monument marks the position held by Pennington's horse artillerists during the entire battle. Behind you, along the Hanover Road, is the monument to the 1st Maine Cavalry, which was kept in reserve supporting the Union artillery. The 1st Maine was not engaged in the fighting, but it still played an important role, representing General Gregg's last possible reserve and the only Federal force remaining at the crossroads. A trooper of the 1st Maine was also the only member of David Gregg's division killed in action during the fighting for East Cavalry Field. The farm house and barn across the road (the Joseph Spangler farm) mark the starting points for the charges of the 1st and 7th Michigan Cavalry Regiments. Get back in your car and turn right on the Hanover Road (Pa. State Route 116) (GPS BENCHMARK 20).

The 1st Maine Cavalry Monument (top)
and the Joseph Spangler farm buildings (bottom).

Author

Rank's Battery Monument

Travel west on the Hanover Road for .1 of a mile (GPS BENCHMARK 21). You will find the monument to Capt. William D. Rank's Battery H, 3rd Pennsylvania Heavy Artillery, placed on the spot where Rank's gunners set up during the fight for Brinkerhoff's Ridge on July 2. Fire from these guns saved Dr. Tate and hospital steward Walter Kempster. The fire also slowed

The 3rd Pennsylvania Heavy Artillery (Rank's Battery) Monument.

Author

the 2nd Virginia Infantry just enough to enable the 3rd Pennsylvania troopers to beat them to the stone wall. Victory in the fighting on July 2 hinged on control of that wall. These guns were not present during the fighting on July 3.

The 16th Pennsylvania Cavalry Monument

Continue west on the Hanover Road (Pa. State Route 116). The older house immediately to the right of the road just west of the monument to Rank's battery is the Abraham Reever house. You will also pass over Cress Run. The older house just on the west side of Cress Run is the John Cress house.

Travel a total of 1.5 miles. Just after you pass under the Route 15 bypass, you will see two turns to the left. Take the second left turn onto Highland Avenue (GPS BENCHMARK 22). Continue along Highland Avenue for .4 of a mile until you come to the monument of the 16th Pennsylvania Cavalry of Col. J. Irvin Gregg's brigade (GPS BENCHMARK 23). This monument receives very little visitation. It marks the end of Irvin Gregg's picket line, which connected with Brig. Gen. Thomas Neill's Sixth Corps infantry brigade, posted on nearby Wolf's Hill. This position is significant, as it demonstrates how well David Gregg had protected the flanks and rear of the Army of the Potomac on July 3, 1863. Turn around and return .4 of a mile to the Hanover Road and turn left (GPS BENCHMARK 24).

Return to the Museum and Visitor's Center:
The End of the Tour

Travel 1.6 miles to the intersection of the Hanover Road (Pa. State Route 116) and U.S. Route 30 (GPS BENCHMARK 25). Continue west on Route 30 for .2 of a mile to the town square (GPS BENCHMARK 26). Turn left onto Baltimore Street at the town square and continue south on Baltimore Street for 1.4 miles and turn right into the entrance for the Visitor Center (GPS BENCHMARK 27). Return to the Visitor Center (GPS BENCHMARK 28). Your tour of the fights for Brinkerhoff's Ridge and East Cavalry Field ends here. You will have covered a total of 13.7 miles.

The 16th Pennsylvania Cavalry Monument.

Author

If you have followed these directions carefully, you will have seen both battlefields in their entirety. Hopefully, you have enjoyed your tour, and you have come away from it with a greater understanding of the fighting that took place there.

GPS Benchmarks

BENCHMARK 1: W39° 48.659"
N077° 13.451"

BENCHMARK 2: N39° 48.731"
W077° 13.302"

BENCHMARK 3: N39° 49.587"
W077° 13.851"

BENCHMARK 4: N39° 49.858"
W077° 13.570"

BENCHMARK 5: N39° 49.343"
W077° 11.424"

BENCHMARK 6: N39° 49.293"
W077° 11.207"

BENCHMARK 7: N39° 49.370"
W077° 11.139"

BENCHMARK 8: N39° 50.472"
W077° 10.334"

BENCHMARK 9: N39° 50.429"
W077° 10.254"

BENCHMARK 10: N39° 50.303"
W077° 10.028"

BENCHMARK 11: N39° 50.023"
W077° 10.305"

BENCHMARK 12: N39° 49.720"
W077° 10.204"

BENCHMARK 13: N39° 49.669"
W077° 10.091"

BENCHMARK 14: N39° 49.600"
W077° 09.902"

BENCHMARK 15: N39° 49.561"
W077° 09.795"

BENCHMARK 16: N39° 49.443"
W077° 09.637"

BENCHMARK 17: N39° 49.342"
W077° 09.700"

BENCHMARK 18: N39° 49.283"
W077° 09.891"

BENCHMARK 19: N39° 49.144"
W077° 10.116"

BENCHMARK 20: N39° 49.100"
W077° 10.160"

BENCHMARK 21: N39° 49.079"
W077° 10.178"

BENCHMARK 22: N39° 49.127"
W077° 10.383"

BENCHMARK 23: N39° 49.499"
W077° 11.990"

BENCHMARK 24: N39° 49.058"
W077° 11.868"

BENCHMARK 25: N39° 49.499"
W077° 11.980"

BENCHMARK 26: N39° 49.858"
W077° 13.570"

BENCHMARK 27: N39° 49.857"
W077° 13.851"

BENCHMARK 28: N39° 48.659"
W077° 13.451"

Bibliography

PRIMARY SOURCES:

Newspapers

Martinsburg Independent
The National Tribune
New York Times
Philadelphia North American
Philadelphia Weekly Times
Raleigh News & Observer
Richmond Daily Dispatch

Government Publications

The War of the Rebellion: A Compilation of the Official Records of the Union and Confederate Armies. 128 volumes in 3 series. Washington, D.C.: United States Government Printing Office, 1889.

Unpublished Manuscripts

Bentley Historical Library, University of Michigan, Ann Arbor, Michigan:
 Russell A. Alger Papers
 William Baird Memoirs
 John Ball Letters
 Andrew N. Buck Papers
 John A. Clark Papers
 Victor E. Comte Letters
 Edward Corselius Letters
 John B. Kay Letters
 O'Brien Family Papers

Christopher Densmore Collection, Getzville, New York:
 Daniel Townsend Diary

Gettysburg National Military Park, Gettysburg, Pennsylvania:
    Edward Brugh letter, April 27, 1886
    Andrew Newton Buck letter of July 9, 1863
    William G. Delony letter, July 4, 1863
    Thomas W. Ferry letter, August 3, 1863
    Account of Lt. Gaines, 14th Virginia Cavalry
    Dexter Macomber diary for 1863
    William Hope Peek letter, July 8, 1863
    Noble D. Preston letter of March 5, 1896
    Undated letter by Luther S. Trowbridge
    Walter Kempster, M.D., to My Ever Dearest Beloved One, July 10, 1863

Historical Society of Pennsylvania, Philadelphia, Pennsylvania:
    William Brooke-Rawle Papers
    Newhall Family Papers

Library of Congress, Manuscripts Division, Washington, D. C.:
    David McMurtrie Gregg Papers

The National Archives, Washington, D. C.:
    RG 94, Union Battle Reports
    William E. Miller Medal of Honor file, RG 94,
    Entry No. 496, Box 1391

Perkins Library, Duke University, Durham, North Carolina:
    Stephens Calhoun Smith Papers

Dona Sauerburger Collection, Gambrills, Maryland:
    Thomas Lucas Letters

United States Army Heritage and Education Center, Carlisle, Pennsylvania:
    Robert Brake Collection
    Civil War Times Illustrated Collection
    Harrisburg Civil War Roundtable Collection
    Lewis Leigh Collection

United States Military Academy, Special Collections, West Point,
New York:
    George A. Custer Papers

Wilson Library, Southern Historical Collection, University of North
Carolina, Chapel Hill, North Carolina:
    Marcus Lafayette Burnett Papers
    Philip St. George Cooke Papers
    Peek Family Papers
    Charles S. Venable Papers
    Joseph F. Waring Papers

Published Sources

1886 History of Adams County Pennsylvania. Chicago: Warner, Beers Co., 1886.

Beale, George W. "General Wade Hampton: Tribute from a Virginian who Served Under Him." *Richmond Dispatch*, May 4, 1902.

Beale, Richard L. T. *History of the Ninth Virginia Cavalry in the War Between the States*. Richmond: B. H. Johnson Co., 1899.

Bigelow, John A. "Draw Saber, Charge!" *The National Tribune*, May 27, 1886.

Blackford, William W. *War Years with JEB Stuart*. New York: Charles Scribner's Sons, 1945.

Bouldin, Edward E. "Charlotte Cavalry: A Brief History of the Gallant Command." *Richmond Dispatch*, May 28, 1899.

Brooke-Rawle, William, ed. *History of the Third Pennsylvania Cavalry in the American Civil War of 1861-1865*. Philadelphia: Franklin Printing Co., 1905.

Brooks, Ulysses R. *Stories of the Confederacy*. Columbia, SC: State Publishing Co., The State Co., 1912.

Carpenter, J. Edward. "Gregg's Cavalry at Gettysburg," included in *Annals of the War: Written by Leading Participants North & South*. Philadelphia: Philadelphia Weekly Times Publishing Co., 1879.

Carpenter, James L. "My Experience at Gettysburg," included in William O. Lee, comp. *Personal and Historical Sketches and Facial History of and by Members of the Seventh Regiment Michigan Volunteer Cavalry 1862-1865*. Detroit, MI: Ralston-Stroup Printing Co., 1904.

Carter, William R. *Sabres, Saddles, and Spurs*. Walbrook D. Swank, ed. Shippensburg, PA: Burd Street Press, 1998.

Cauthen, Charles E., ed. *Family Letters of the Three Wade Hamptons, 1782-1901*. Columbia: University of South Carolina Press, 1953.

Cooke, John Esten. *Wearing of the Gray; Being Personal Portraits, Scenes and Adventures of the War*. New York: E.B. Treat & Co., 1867.

Cooper, Rev. David M. *Obituary Discourse on Occasion of the Death of Noah Henry Ferry, Major of the Fifth Michigan Cavalry, Killed at Gettysburg, July 3, 1863*. New York: John F. Trow, 1863.

Cummins, Edmund H. "The Signal Corps in the Confederate States Army," *Southern Historical Society Papers*, 16 (1888), 93-107.

Custer, Elizabeth Bacon. *Tenting on the Plains, or General Custer in Kansas and Texas*. Norman: University of Oklahoma Press, 1971.

D'Aguilar, Lieut. Gen. Sir G. G., trans. *Napoleon's Art of War*. New York: Barnes & Noble, 1995.

Doster, William E. *Lincoln and Episodes of the Civil War*. New York: G. P. Putnam's Sons, 1915.

Douglas, Henry Kyd. *I Rode with Stonewall: The War Experiences of the Youngest Member of Jackson's Staff*. Chapel Hill: University of North Carolina Press, 1968.

Gibbon, John. *The Artillerist's Manual, Compiled from Various Sources and Adapted to the Service of the United States*. New York: D. Van Nostrand, 1860.

Gibson, William. "Address of Captain William Gibson," included in *Report of the State of Maryland Gettysburg Monument Commission to His Excellency E. E. Jackson, Governor of Maryland, June 17th, 1891.* Baltimore: William K. Boyle & Son, 1891: 101-105.

Gilmore, David M. "Cavalry: Its Use and Value as Illustrated by Reference to the Engagements of Kelly's Ford and Gettysburg," *Military Order of the Loyal Legion of the United States, Minnesota Commandery, Glimpses of the Nation's Struggle,* 2nd series.

————. "With General Gregg at Gettysburg," Glimpses of the Nation's Struggle, 4th Series, Military Order of the Loyal Legion of the United States, Minnesota Commandery, Read October 3, 1893.

Goldsborough, W. W. *The Maryland Line in the Confederate Army.* Baltimore: Guggenheimer, Weil & Co., 1900.

Graham, William A., Jr. "From Brandy Station to the Heights of Gettysburg," *The News and Observer,* February 7, 1904.

Gregg, David M. *The Second Cavalry Division of the Army of the Potomac in the Gettysburg Campaign.* Philadelphia: privately published, 1907.

Haden, B. J. *Reminiscences of J.E.B. Stuart's Cavalry.* Charlottesville, VA: Progress Publishing Co., n.d.

Hagadorn, Dewitt C. "The 10th NY Cav.—Porter Guard: The Great Cavalry Battle on the Right at Gettysburg," *The National Tribune,* January 25, 1906.

Harris, Nathaniel E. *Autobiography: The Story of an Old Man's Life with Reminiscences of Seventy-Five Years.* Macon, GA: J. W. Burke Co., 1925.

Harris, Samuel. *The Michigan Brigade of Cavalry at the Battle of Gettysburg.* Cass City, MI: Co. A, 5th Michigan Cavalry, 1894.

"How Another Flag Went Through," *The National Tribune,* April 13, 1892.

Howard, Wiley C. *Sketches of Cobb Legion Cavalry and Some Incidents and Scenes Remembered.* Privately published, 1901.

Hudgins, Garland C. and Richard B. Kleese, eds. *Recollections of an Old Dominion Dragoon: The Civil War Experiences of Sgt. Robert S. Hudgins II, Co. B, 3rd Virginia Cavalry.* Orange, VA: Publisher's Press, 1993.

Husby, Karla Jean, comp. and ed., Eric J. Wittenberg. *Under Custer's Command: The Civil War Journal of James Henry Avery.* Washington, D.C.: Brassey's, 2000.

Imboden, John D. "The Confederate Retreat from Gettysburg," included in Robert U. Johnson and Clarence C. Buel, eds. *Battles and Leaders of the Civil War.* 4 vols. New York: The Century Co. 1888. 3:420-429.

"In Memoriam Charles Treichel," *The Cavalry Society of the United States.* Concord, NH: published by the Society, 1894, 280-283.

Isham, Asa B. *An Historical Sketch of the Seventh Regiment Michigan Volunteer Cavalry, from Its Organization, in 1862, to Its Muster Out, in 1865.* New York: Town Topics Publishing Co., 1892.

Jones, Terry L., ed. *Campbell Brown's Civil War: With Ewell and the Army of Northern Virginia.* Baton Rouge: Louisiana State University Press, 2001.

Kempster, Walter, M.D. "The Cavalry at Gettysburg," *War Papers, Vol. 4, Military Order of the Loyal Legion of the United States, Wisconsin Commandery,* Read October 1, 1913.

Kidd, James H. *Personal Recollections of a Cavalryman in Custer's Michigan Brigade.* Ionia, MI: Sentinel Publishing Co., 1908.

Klement, Frank L., ed. "Edwin B. Bigelow: A Michigan Sergeant in the Civil War," *Michigan History*, 38 (Sept. 1954).

Ladd, David L. and Audrey J., eds. *The Bachelder Papers*. 3 vols. Dayton, OH: Morningside, 1994.

———. *John Bachelder's History of the Battle of Gettysburg*. Dayton, OH: Morningside, 1997.

Malone, P. J. "Charge of Black's Cavalry Regiment at Gettysburg," *Southern Historical Society Papers*, 16 (1888).

Matteson, Ron, ed. *Civil War Campaigns of the 10th New York Cavalry With One Soldier's Personal Correspondence*. Lulu.com: 2007.

McClellan, Henry B. *The Life and Campaigns of Major-General J.E.B. Stuart*. Boston: Houghton, Mifflin & Co., 1883.

Meyer, Henry C. *Civil War Experiences Under Bayard, Gregg, Kilpatrick, Custer, Raulston, and Newberry 1862, 1863, 1864*. New York: privately published, 1911.

Michigan at Gettysburg, July 1st, 2nd, and 3rd, 1863. Detroit: Winn & Hammond, 1889.

Miller, William E. "The Cavalry Battle Near Gettysburg," included in Robert U. Johnson and Clarence C. Buel, eds. *Battles and Leaders of the Civil War*. 4 vols. New York: The Century Co. 1888. 3:397-406.

Mingus, Scott L., Sr., ed. *Human Interest Stories of the Gettysburg Campaign*, Vol. II. Gettysburg, PA: Colecraft Industries, 2007.

Mohr, James C., ed. *The Cormany Diaries: A Northern Family in the Civil War*. Pittsburgh: University of Pittsburgh Press, 1982.

Morgan, William A. "Desperate Charges: The First Virginia Cavalry at Gettysburg." *Richmond Dispatch*, April 9, 1899.

Mosby, John Singleton. *Stuart's Cavalry in the Gettysburg Campaign*. New York: Moffat, Yard & Co., 1908.

Murray, Elizabeth Dunbar. *My Mother Used to Say: A Natchez Belle of the Sixties*. Boston: Christopher Publishing House, 1959.

Nanzig, Thomas P., ed. *The Civil War Memoirs of a Virginia Cavalryman: Lt. Robert T. Hubard, Jr.* Tuscaloosa: University of Alabama Press, 2007.

Newhall, Frederick C. *With General Sheridan in Lee's Last Campaign*. Philadelphia: J. B. Lippincott, 1866.

New York Monuments Commission for the Battlefields of Gettysburg and Chattanooga: Final Report on the Battlefield of Gettysburg. 3 vols. Albany, NY: J. B. Lyon Co., 1902.

"Obituary of John Quincy Adams Nadenbousch," *Martinsburg Independent*, September 17, 1892.

d'Orleans, Louis Phillipe Albert, Comte de Paris. *History of the Civil War in America*. 3 vols. Philadelphia: Porter & Coates, 1883.

Paul, E. A. "Operations of Our Cavalry: The Michigan Cavalry Brigade," *New York Times*, August 6, 1863.

Peck, Rufus H. *Reminiscences of a Confederate Soldier of Company C, 2nd Virginia Cavalry*. Fincastle, VA: privately published, 1913.

Pennsylvania at Gettysburg. 2 vols. Harrisburg, PA: B. Slingerly, 1904.

Preston, Noble D. *History of the Tenth Regiment of Cavalry, New York State Volunteers*. New York: D. Appleton & Co., 1892.

Purifoy, John. "Stuart's Cavalry Battle at Gettysburg," *Confederate Veteran*, 28 (1924): 260-263.

Pyne, Henry R. *The History of the First New Jersey Cavalry*. Trenton: J.A. Beecher, 1871.

Rea, D. B. *Sketches of Hampton's Cavalry, Embracing the Principal Exploits of the Cavalry in the Campaigsns of 1862 and 1863*. Columbia, SC: South Carolinian Steam Press, 1864.

Robertson, John, comp. *Michigan in the War*. Lansing: W. S. George & Co., 1882.

Rodenbough, Theophilus F. "Cavalry War Lessons," *Journal of the United States Cavalry Association*, 2 (June 1889): 101-123.

Ronemus, Nancy, ed. "Eyewitness to War," *America's Civil War* (March 1997).

Samito, Christian G., ed. *Commanding Boston's Irish Ninth: The Civil War Letters of Colonel Patrick R. Guiney, Ninth Massachusettes Volunteer Infantry*. New York: Fordham University Press, 1998.

Schuricht, Hermann. "Jenkins' Brigade in the Gettysburg Campaign," *The Richmond Dispatch*, April 5, 1896.

Scott, John Zachary Holladay. "John Zachary Holladay Scott, Confederate Soldier 1861-1865," included in *Confederate Reminiscences and Letters 1861-1865*. vol. 7. Georgia Division United Daughters of the Confederacy, Atlanta GA: 1998: 127-157.

Speese, Andrew Jackson. *Story of Companies H, A and C Third Pennsylvania Cavalry at Gettysburg*, July 3, 1863. Philadelphia: privately published, 1907.

Styple, William B. *Generals in Bronze: Interviewing the Commanders of the Civil War*. Kearny, NJ: Belle Grove Publishing, 2005.

Tidball, John C. "Artillery Service in the War of the Rebellion," Part V, *Journal of the Military Service Institution of the United States*, 13 (July 1892): 677-707.

"To Recover the Flag," *The National Tribune*, March 4, 1897.

Tobie, Edward P. "Historical Sketch," included in *Maine at Gettysburg: Report of Maine Commissioners Prepared by the Executive Committee*. Portland, ME: Lakeside Press, 1898: 487-514.

———. *History of the First Maine Cavalry, 1861-1865*. Boston: Press of Emory & Hughes, 1887.

Toombs, Samuel. *New Jersey Troops in the Gettysburg Campaign, From June 5 to July 31, 1863*. Orange, NJ: Evening Mail Publishing House, 1888.

Trout, Robert J., ed. *In the Saddle With Stuart: The Story of Frank Smith Robertson of Jeb Stuart's Staff*. Gettysburg, PA: Thomas Publications, 1998.

———. *Memoirs of the Stuart Horse Artillery Battalion, Vol. 2: Breathed's and McGregor's Batteries*. Knoxville: University of Tennessee Press, 2010.

Trowbridge, Luther S. "The Operations of the Cavalry in the Gettysburg Campaign," *Michigan War Papers, Military Order of the Loyal Legion of the United States*, Vol. 1 (1886): 1-17.

Wells, Edward L. *Hampton and His Cavalry in '64*. Richmond: B. F. Johnson Publishing Co., 1899.

Witcher, Vincent A. "Chambersburg Raid: Another Account of that Thrilling Affair." *Richmond Dispatch*, April 30, 1899.

Wittenberg, Eric J., ed. *At Custer's Side: The Civil War Writings of James Harvey Kidd*. Kent, OH: Kent State University Press, 2001.

————. *One of Custer's Wolverines: The Civil War Letters of Brevet Brigadier General James H. Kidd, 6th Michigan Cavalry.* Kent, OH: Kent State University Press, 2000.

Wright, Catherine M., ed. *Lee's Last Casualty: The Life and Letters of Sgt. Robert W. Parker, Second Virginia Cavalry.* Knoxville: University of Tennessee Press, 2008.

SECONDARY SOURCES

Allardice, Bruce S. *Confederate Colonels: A Biographical Register.* Columbia: University of Missouri Press, 2008.

Andrew, Rod, Jr. *Wade Hampton: Confederate Warrior to Southern Redeemer.* Chapel Hill: University of North Carolina Press, 2008.

Ashe, Samuel A., Stephen B. Weeks, and Charles L. Van Noppen, eds. *Biographical History of North Carolina from Colonial Times to the Present.* 8 vols. Greensboro, NC: Charles L. Van Noppen, 1907.

Bates, Samuel P. *Martial Deeds of Pennsylvania.* Philadelphia: T. H. Davis & Co., 1875.

Beyer, W. F. and O. F. Keydel, eds. *Deeds of Valor: How America's Civil War Heroes Won the Congressional Medal of Honor.* 2 vols. Detroit: Perrien-Keydel Co., 1901.

Bilby, Joseph G. *A Revolution in Arms: A History of the First Repeating Rifles.* Yardley, PA: Westholme Publishing, 2006.

Boatner, Mark M., III. *Civil War Dictionary.* New York: David McKay Co., 1959.

Brennan, Patrick. *"To Die Game": Gen. J. E. B. Stuart, CSA.* Gettysburg, PA: Farnsworth House Military Impressions, 1998.

Burgess, Milton V. *David Gregg: Pennsylvania Cavalryman.* Privately published, 1984.

Busey, John W. and David G. Martin. *Regimental Strengths and Losses at Gettysburg.* Hightstown, NJ: Longstreet House, 1994.

Carhart, Tom. *Lost Triumph: Lee's Real Plan at Gettysburg and Why It Failed.* New York: G. P. Putnam's Sons, 2005.

Cole, Scott C. *34th Battalion Virginia Cavalry.* Lynchburg, VA: H. E. Howard Co., 1993.

"David McMurtrie Gregg," Circular No. 6, Series of 1917, *Military Order of the Loyal Legion of the United States, Commandery of Pennsylvania, May 3, 1917.*

Davis, Burke. *JEB Stuart: The Last Cavalier.* New York: Rinehart & Co., 1959.

Davis, William C. and Julie Hoffman, eds. *The Confederate General.* 6 vols. New York: The National Historical Society, 1991.

Dickinson, Jack L. *Wayne County, West Virginia in the Civil War.* Huntington, WV: privately published, 2003.

Downey, Fairfax. *The Guns at Gettysburg.* New York: Collier Books, 1962.

Driver, Robert, Jr. *1st Virginia Cavalry.* Lynchburg, VA: H. E. Howard Co., 1991.

Faeder, Gustav F. "Horsemen at Gettysburg: While Pickett Made His Charge, Custer Saved the Union," *Civil War,* 8 (July/August 1990), 24-31.

Frye, Dennis E. *2nd Virginia Infantry.* Lynchburg, VA: H. E. Howard Co., 1984.

Gorman, Paul R. "J.E.B. Stuart and Gettysburg," *Gettysburg: Historical Articles of Lasting Interest,* No. 1 (July 1989), 86-92.

Gottfried, Bradley M. *The Artillery of Gettysburg.* Nashville, TN: Cumberland House, 2008.

Hanna, Charles. *Gettysburg Medal of Honor Recipients*. Springville, UT: Bonneville Books, 2010.

Harrell, Roger H. *The 2nd North Carolina Cavalry*. Jefferson, NC: McFarland & Co., 2004.

Hatch, Thom. *Clashes of Cavalry : The Civil War Careers of George Armstrong Custer and Jeb Stuart*. Mechanicsburg, PA: Stackpole, 2001.

———. "Custer vs. Stuart: The Clash at Gettysburg," *Columbiad*, 2 (Summer 1998): 44-60.

Heitman, Francis B. *Historical Register and Dictionary of the United States Army, from Its Organization September 29, 1789 to March 2, 1903*. 2 vols. Washington, DC: United States Government Printing Office, 1903.

Holland, Lynnwood E. *Pierce M. B. Young: The Warwick of the South*. Athens: University of Georgia Press, 1964.

Hopkins, Donald A. *The Little Jeff: The Jeff Davis Legion, Cavalry, Army of Northern Virginia*. Shippensburg, PA: White Mane, 1999.

Kesterson, Brian Stuart. *Campaigning with the 17th Virginia Cavalry: Night Hawks at Monocacy*. Washington, WV: Night Hawk Press, 2005.

Krick, Robert K. *Lee's Colonels: A Biographical Register of the Field Officers of the Army of Northern Virginia*. 4th ed. Dayton, OH: Morningside, 1992.

Krolick, Marshall D. "Forgotten Field: The Cavalry Battle East of Gettysburg on July 3, 1863," *Gettysburg: Historical Articles of Lasting Interest*, No. 4 (January 1991): 75-88.

Logan, Andy. *The Man Who Robbed the Robber Barons: The Story of Colonel William d'Alton Mann: War Hero, Profiteer, Inventor, and Blackmailer Extraordinary*. New York: W. W. Norton, 1965.

Longacre, Edward G. *The Cavalry at Gettysburg: A Tactical Study of Mounted Operations During the Civil War's Pivotal Campaign, 9 June-14 July 1863*. Rutherford, NJ: Fairleigh-Dickinson University Press, 1986.

———. *Custer and His Wolverines: The Michigan Cavalry Brigade 1861-1865*. Conshohocken, PA: Combined, 1997.

———. *Fitz Lee: A Military Biography of Major General Fitzhugh Lee, C.S.A.* New York: DaCapo Press, 2005.

———. *Jersey Cavaliers: A History of the First New Jersey Volunteer Cavalry, 1861-1865*. Hightstown, NJ: Longstreet House, 1992.

Mesic, Harriett Bey. *Cobb's Legion Cavalry: A History and Roster of the Ninth Georgia Volunteers in the Civil War*. Jefferson, NC: McFarland & Co., 2009.

Monaghan, Jay. *Custer: The Life of General George Armstrong Custer*. Boston: Little, Brown & Co., 1959.

Nesbitt, Mark. *Saber and Scapegoat: J.E.B. Stuart and the Gettysburg Controversy*. Mechanicsburg, PA: Stackpole, 1994.

Newton, George. *Silent Sentinels: A Reference Guide to the Artillery at Gettysburg*. El Dorado Hills, CA: Savas Beatie, 2005.

Nichols, James L. *General Fitzhugh Lee: A Biography*. Lynchburg, VA: H. E. Howard Co., 1989.

O'Brien, Kevin E. "'Glory Enough for All': Lt. William Brooke-Rawle and the 3rd Pennsylvania Cavalry at Gettysburg," *Gettysburg: Historical Articles of Lasting Interest*, No. 13 (July 1995): 89-107.

Petruzzi, J. David and Steven Stanley. *The Complete Gettysburg Guide: Walking and Driving Tours of the Battlefield, Town, Cemeteries, Field Hospital Sites, and other Topics of Historical Interest*. El Dorado Hills, CA: Savas Beatie, 2009.

Pfanz, Harry W. *Gettysburg: Culp's Hill & Cemetery Hill*. Chapel Hill: University of North Carolina Press, 1993.

Phipps, Michael. *"Come On You Wolverines!": Custer at Gettysburg*. Gettysburg, PA: Farnsworth House Military Impressions, 1995.

Riggs, David F. *East of Gettysburg: Stuart vs. Custer*. Bellevue, NE: Olde Army Press, 1970.

Rodenbough, Theophilus F. *The Bravest Five Hundred of '61: Their Noble Deeds Described by Themselves, Together with an Account of Some Gallant Exploits of Our Soldiers in Indian Warfare. How the Medal of Honor was Won*. New York: G. W. Dillingham, 1891.

Rowell, John W. *Yankee Artillerymen: Through the Civil War with Eli Lilly's Indiana Battery*. Knoxville: University of Tennessee Press, 1975.

Rummel, George A., III. *72 Days at Gettysburg: Organization of the 10th Regiment, New York Volunteer Cavalry*. Shippensburg, PA: White Mane, 1997.

Shevchuk, Paul M. "The Fight for Brinkerhoff's Ridge, July 2, 1863," *Gettysburg: Historical Articles of Lasting Interest*, No. 2 (January 1990): 61-74.

———. "The Lost Hours of 'JEB' Stuart," *Gettysburg: Historical Articles of Lasting Interest*, No. 4 (January 1991): 65-74.

———. "The Wounding of Albert Jenkins, July 2, 1863," *Gettysburg: Historical Articles of Lasting Interest*, No. 3 (July 1990), 51-63.

Smith, Timothy H., comp. *Farms at Gettysburg: The Fields of Battle*. Gettysburg, PA: Thomas Publications, 2007.

Starr, Stephen Z. *The Union Cavalry in the Civil War*. 3 vols. Baton Rouge: Louisiana State University Press, 1979.

Stowe, Mark S. *Company B, 6th Michigan Cavalry*. Grand Rapids, MI: privately published, 2000.

Thomas, Emory M. *Bold Dragoon: The Life of J.E.B. Stuart*. New York: Harper & Row, 1986.

Thomason, John W., Jr. *Jeb Stuart*. New York: Charles Scribner's Sons, 1929.

Toalson, Jeff, ed. *Send a Pair of Old Boots & Kiss My Little Girls: The Civil War Letters of Richard and Mary Watkins, 1861-1865*. New York: iUniverse, 2009.

Toomey, Daniel Carroll and Charles Albert Earp. *Marylanders in Blue: The Artillery and the Cavalry*. Baltimore: Toomey Press, 1999.

Trout, Robert J. *Galloping Thunder: The Stuart Horse Artillery Battalion*. Mechanicsburg, PA: Stackpole, 2002.

Urwin, Gregory J. W. *Custer Victorious: The Civil War Battles of General George Armstrong Custer*. East Brunswick, NJ: Associated University Presses, 1983.

Walker, Paul D. *The Cavalry Battle that Saved the Union: Custer vs. Stuart at Gettysburg*. Gretna, LA: Pelican Publishing Co., 2002.

Warner, Ezra J. *Generals in Blue: The Lives of the Union Commanders*. Baton Rouge: Louisiana State University Press, 1964.

———. *Generals in Gray: The Lives of the Confederate Commanders*. Baton Rouge: Louisiana State University Press, 1959.

Wellman, Manly. *Giant in Gray: A Biography of Wade Hampton of South Carolina.* New York: Charles Scribner's Sons, 1949.

Wert, Jeffry D. *Cavalryman of the Lost Cause: A Biography of J.E.B. Stuart.* New York: Simon and Schuster, 2008.

————. *Custer: The Controversial Life of George Armstrong Custer.* New York: Simon & Schuster, 1996.

————. *Gettysburg: Day Three.* New York: Simon & Schuster, 2001.

Wister, Sally Butler. *Walter S. Newhall: A Memoir.* Philadelphia: The Sanitary Commission, 1864.

Wittenberg, Eric J. *Gettysburg's Forgotten Cavalry Actions: Farnsworth's Charge, South Cavalry Field and the Battle of Fairfield, July 3, 1863.* El Dorado Hills, CA: Savas Beatie, 2011.

————. "The Truth About the Withdrawal of Brig. Gen. John Buford's Cavalry, July 2, 1863," *The Gettysburg Magazine*, 37 (July 2007): 71-82.

Wittenberg, Eric J. and J. David Petruzzi, *Plenty of Blame to Go Around: Jeb Stuart's Controversial Ride to Gettysburg.* El Dorado Hills, CA: Savas Beatie, 2006.

Wittenberg, Eric J., J. David Petruzzi, and Michael F. Nugent, *One Continuous Fight: The Retreat from Gettysburg and the Pursuit of Lee's Army of Northern Virginia, July 4-14, 1863.* El Dorado Hills, CA: Savas Beatie, 2008.

Index